Machine Embroidery & Textile Decoration

Inspirational Projects for Creative Clothing and Accessories

Elli Woodsford

APPLE

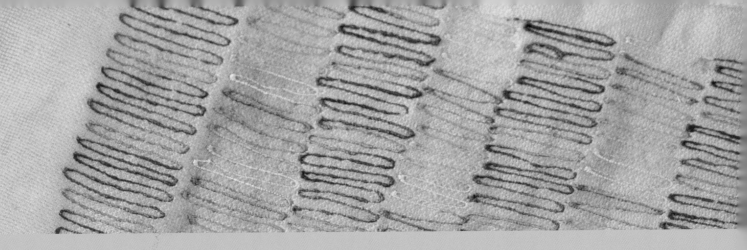

First published in the UK
By Apple Press in 2006
Sheridan House
114 Western Road
Hove
East Sussex
BN3 IDD

www.apple-press.com

ISBN-10: 1-84543-117-0
ISBN-13: 978-1-84543-117-4

10 9 8 7 6 5 4 3 2 1

Design: Yee Design
Cover Image and photography: Allan Penn Photography
Technical Editor: Susan Huxley
Copy Editor: Katherine O. Riess
Patterns: Roberta Frauwirth
Illustrations: Lainé Roundy

Printed in Singapore

INTRODUCTION

THIS BOOK IS ABOUT CREATING INDIVIDUAL ACCESSORIES using fabric colouring and machine embroidery. Each chapter contains step-by-step instructions showing basic techniques. These techniques can then be applied to projects that are also in this book. You'll find a belt, handbags, a hat, jackets, shoes and a wrap. When needed, patterns are included for the projects.

All the projects feature machine embroidery techniques that can be accomplished on a basic sewing machine that can perform straight, zigzag and a few additional pattern stitches. The materials lists do not include a sewing machine and iron because it is assumed that you already have these tools at the ready.

Chapter 1 contains four fabric colouration techniques and suggests suitable fabrics for each. It is great fun to colour your own fabric, but I do realize that not everyone has the inclination, space or time. All the projects in Chapter 2 onward can be made using commercially dyed and printed fabrics.

Whether you choose to dye or not, you will need to think about colour. Look at your wardrobe and decide on an accent colour scheme. Decide which fabrics you like and research machine embroidery threads that will complement your chosen palette.

At every stage in this book you will be encouraged to make samples before starting a project. I recommend keeping detailed records of all this information—colour schemes and swatches from your dyeing and colouring experiments. I like to use the swatch card method, an idea borrowed from the fashion industry. Swatch cards are simple to make and store, and will be very useful for reference as you continue to create and try different techniques. Decide to work in either imperial or metric measurements. Never mix the two. The next pages will give you some ideas on how to start making and saving your samples.

MAKING SAMPLES AND RECORDING INFORMATION

As you do this kind of fabric decoration work, recording information is very important. I have numerous samples from my early days of stitching and textile decoration, and have not a clue as to how I achieved the effects. I was convinced I would remember. I did not, and you will not. Write down everything. The time invested in keeping track of your projects will be repaid over and over again.

Be sure to keep two samples: a swatch of the unwashed fabric with measurements and fibre content as far as you know it, and also a washed sample (with measurements), which may show colour loss or a change in the hand (drape) of the fabric. Even if you know the fibre content of the fabrics you buy, always do a wash test first, as laundering and wear inevitably change the characteristics. I scour Indian markets for fabrics. Yet, however exciting the fabrics that I purchase, I resist the temptation to start stitching immediately. This is particularly important if you are going to need to wash the finished item. But even if not, it is good practice to do wash samples and record the results.

OPPOSITE

Handmade header cards on swatches are used to record information needed to achieve the effect again: colour studies, decoration and stitch techniques and fabric types.

OPPOSITE (BELOW)

These are colour studies. Look in magazines for fashion colour schemes that appeal to you. Make a collage of colours and shapes to inspire and provide visual themes for future projects.

GETTING STARTED

1. Start with an A4 (8¹/2" x 11" [21.6 x 27.9 cm]) sheet of card stock to make four header cards for swatches of colour or thread studies, fabric, paper or a combination of these elements. Cut the sheet in half across the 8¹/2" (21.6 cm) width, and then cut each half in half, across the width again.

2. Fold each of the four quarters in half. These are the header cards. Each one is 8¹/2" (21.6 cm) wide, and about 1³/8" (3.5 cm) from a cut edge to the fold.

3. Record all the important information (such as dye or paint used, fabric type, machine tension, stitch techniques, threads used) and any other relevant details on the header card.

4. Place the swatch into the fold inside the header card. Staple through the layers to secure the swatch.

5. Mark and then punch 2 holes through the cardboard so that the swatch can be stored in an A5 (7" x 9" [17.8 x 22.9 cm]) ring binder.

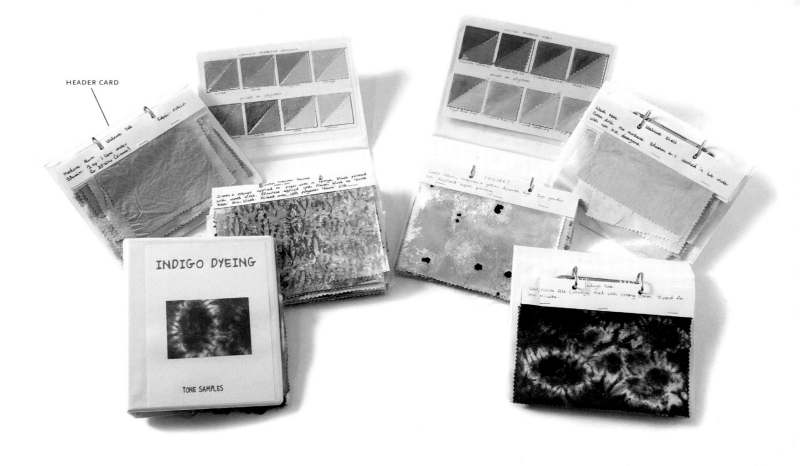

HEADER CARD

INDIGO DYEING

TONE SAMPLES

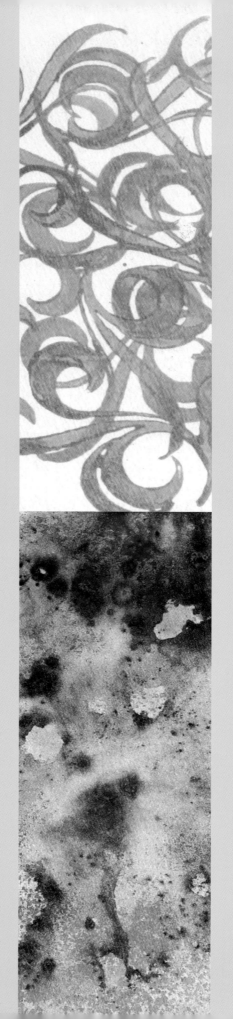

STARTING FROM SCRATCH:
CHOOSING AND COLOURING FABRIC

DYEING OR PAINTING FABRICS IS THE BEST WAY TO
learn about colour: how the primaries (blue, red and yellow)
combine to make new colours, the intricacies of shades and tints
and the way that hues fight or complement one another.

Creating your own colour schemes on a variety of fabrics using
dyes, indigo, paints and walnut ink allows you to be really
creative from the start to the finish of your project. Take time to
experiment. Record everything you do; failures are as important
as successes.

Cotton muslin.
Swirl block
Scarlet + Yellow Dye·Na·Flow.   • Bas Relief Painting   —

Heart Block.   • Bas Relief Painting
100% cotton muslin.   Paints: Violet + magenta Jacquard Dye·Na
Flow.

Square block.   • Bas Relief Painting.
Cotton muslin.
Brick + Violet DyeNaFlow.   —

Fabric: cotton muslin.   • Bas·relief painting   Jacquard
Block: Foam   Paints: Sun Yellow 801   Dye·na·Flow
Side: Right   Turquoise 813

Fabric: 100% 'faux' silk.   • Bas Relief Painting
Paints: Deka Iron On applied to paper with a block. Same block
Used for   Bas relief technique.

Fabric: 100% polyester 'faux' silk   • Bas·relief
Paints: Deka Iron on: Pink 474
with a block + printed. Jacquard
809 + 801 Bas·relief technique.

Fabric: cotton muslin   • Bas·relief painting
Block: Foam   Paints: Sun Yellow 801
Side: Wrong   Turquoise 813   Jacquard
Dye·Na·Flow

Colouring Fabric by Transfer Printing

This method involves colouring a piece of paper with transfer dyes and then transferring the colour to fabric. It is an easy way of applying colour to synthetic fabrics. Suitable materials need to be at least 50 percent synthetic, although the best results are achieved with 100 percent synthetic fibres. Good fabrics to use are acrylic felt, nylon, polyester and polyester cotton. The most vibrant colour transfers happen on polyester satin fabric, which has a shiny surface.

MATERIALS

* office paper
* transfer paint: disperse dye powders, crayons or ready-mixed paints
* printing block (stamp)
* paintbrush
* blow-dryer
* iron

Transfer dye is available as powders, ready-mixed paints and sets of crayons. The powder, which is a disperse dye, is the most versatile, but the crayons and ready-mixed paints are simpler to use.

1. Choose a sheet of white bond (common, uncoated office) paper that has a weight (thickness) of approximately 20–24 pounds (about 80 gsm). If the paper is too thick, the colour will not transfer properly.

2. If needed for the application technique, prepare the transfer paint and paper. Disperse dye powder can be sprinkled dry onto wet paper or dry onto dry paper and then sprayed with water. It can also be placed on paper after it is mixed with water to an inklike consistency, or thickened to the consistency of oil paint. The dye manufacturer supplies the thickener. Ready-mixed paints can be thinned with water but no thickeners are supplied as they are thick enough as is. Crayons can be used on dry or wet paper.

3. Using a paintbrush, printing block (stamp) or sponge, apply the colour in your chosen design. Leave the paper to dry, or speed the process with a blow-dryer.

4. Place the fabric faceup on an ironing board with the coloured paper facedown on top. Press with a hot iron, putting as much pressure as possible on the layers. After about 20 seconds, gently lift the corner of the paper to check the colour on the fabric. If it is not bright enough, iron longer.

5. When satisfied with the results, remove the iron and the paper.

TIP

A clamshell press gives great results, but do cover the base with paper to protect it from any dye that may leak through.

LEFT

Note the colours used, the fabric type and the ironing time. Keep this information with the paper. The paper can be used two or three more times, although the colour will weaken after each transfer. These samples were created with Deka IronOn, a ready-mix transfer paint.

LEFT

Before transferring a design, you can play with the image you create. Colour the paper, tear it into strips, overlap the pieces on the fabric and then complete the transfer process. The transfer dyes are transparent so they can be overlaid.

Using Fabric Paint Techniques

When choosing paints for fabric decoration, I start by buying the most useful colours: lemon yellow, turquoise, magenta, golden yellow, ultramarine blue and brilliant red. From these six colours, it is possible to mix a wide variety of colours. Combining red and yellow yields orange; red and blue makes purple; and blue and yellow leads to green. Then the newest (called secondary) colours can be combined with each other—or the primaries (blue, red and yellow)—to make even more colours.

Later, you may want to expand your paint collection to include black, brick, ecru and violet. These are useful for mixing with both primary and secondary colours.

One of the best reference tools you can create is a colour wheel. You can make two personalized versions using the first six colours that you purchase.

The projects in this book were created with Jacquard Dye-Na-Flow fabric paints, but any thin fabric or silk paint works well. Make sure that you buy runny paints, or water down any thick ones. The wheel above, top, was created with Magenta 809, Turquoise 813 and Sun Yellow 801. The wheel shown above, bottom, features combinations of Brilliant Red 806, Cerulean Blue 815 and Golden Yellow 802.

MATERIALS

* cotton muslin
  (a fine, open-weave fabric)
* paper
* fabric paints
* glue
* scissors
* iron

1. Cut cotton muslin (or other favored fabric) into 9 pieces, each 3" (7.5 cm) square.

2. Set aside the lemon yellow, turquoise and magenta paints to make the second colour wheel. Continue the following steps to make the first colour wheel with the remaining paint colours: golden yellow, ultramarine blue and brilliant red.

3. Colour one fabric square with each of the three paints, apply heat to make the paint permanent (if necessary per manufacturer's instructions) and set the pieces aside to dry.

4. On a piece of thick paper, draw a circle with a 4" (10 cm) diameter. Divide this circle into 12 pie-shaped sections.

5. Cut a matching pie shape from each of the three coloured fabrics. Using the drawn lines as guides, glue these shapes inside the colour wheel so that there are three shapes between each swatch.

6. Mix together small, equal amounts of the brilliant red and ultramarine blue (magenta and turquoise for the second wheel). The result is violet. Use this to colour another fabric square. Cut a pie shape from the dried fabric and attach it to the emerging colour wheel on the paper. Glue the new shade between the brilliant red and ultramarine blue swatches. Save the violet paint.

7. Combine brilliant red with golden yellow (magenta and lemon yellow for the second swatch) to make orange paint, and golden yellow with ultramarine blue (lemon yellow and turquoise) to make green paint. Use these colours to make pie-shaped swatches, and glue them between the colours used to make them. Now the secondary colours are attached. Save the orange and green paint.

8. Combining only colours that are side by side on the emerging colour wheel, make and attach the remaining pie shapes.

Little fabric squares of colours are useful for planning colour schemes and looking at colour proportions. If you are ever stuck for a colour to add to a project, place the colour chips and fabric samples on a table and play around until you find a combination that you like. There are two advantages to working like this. First, you don't spend a fortune on colours that you don't need, and second, mixing colours will really sharpen your colour sense.

TECHNIQUE 3

Applying Bas Relief Painting

Experiments with silk and thin (free-flowing, ready-mixed) paints led to this technique. It is very easy, economical with paint and needs little equipment, yet gives fantastic results.

Working on cotton muslin (a fine, open-weave fabric) yields the most dramatic results, but fine silk—both habutai and the polyester faux silk—work really well, too. Painting on heavier fabrics is not as effective, but experiment with what you can find and record your results—even the failures. Something that has an unexpected result can set you off in a different direction!

This technique was used for the Swirl-Painted Wrap project, page 56.

This step-by-step technique uses cotton muslin (a fine, open-weave fabric), Jacquard Dye-Na-Flow fabric paints in brick and turquoise and a foam printing block (stamp). You will also need three fat, strong paintbrushes (the type used for artists' acrylic paints); a water pot; and a salon-quality blow-dryer. The blow-dryer will work hard, so make sure that it is designed to run for lengthy periods.

MATERIALS

* fabric, such as cotton muslin (a fine, open-weave fabric)
* fabric paints
* foam printing block (stamp)
* 3 fat, strong paintbrushes
* blow-dryer
* iron
* plastic sheeting
* pot of clean water

1. Wash the fabric at 104°F (40°C). Let it dry until damp. If you are painting a large area, the fabric will probably dry before you have finished. Do not worry, just dampen the fabric as you continue to work.

2. Cover the work area with plastic sheeting. Choose a foam printing block that has a fairly simple design, with plenty of depth. Place the fabric over the foam block. Dip a fat, strong paintbrush in clean water. Use the brush to push the fabric into the recessed areas of the block.

3. Dip another clean, fat, strong paintbrush into a turquoise paint and gently spread it over the fabric on the printing block's surface. Lightly brush brick-coloured paint into the fabric surface with a new paintbrush.

4. Using the brush that was dipped in the water, mix the paints together on the surface of the fabric, really working the fabric into the block.

TIP

As you work the paint colours together in step 4, keep dipping the mixing brush into the water pot. The water will gradually become a lavender colour. Don't change it. Use this tinted water to continue working the fabric into the recessed areas of the printing block. You will need less paint.

LEFT
Push the damp fabric into the deeper portions of the printing block's pattern, then lightly paint the fabric surface with two different colours.

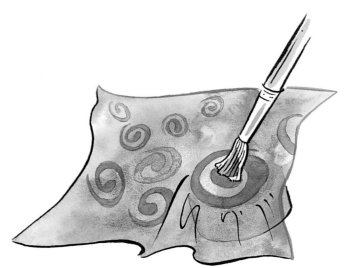

5. Keeping the fabric pushed into the printing block, place the blow-dryer about 1" (2.5 cm) above the fabric surface and switch it on to the hottest setting. Remove the fabric from the printing block when the fabric is dry.

6. Move the printing block to the next area to be painted and repeat the process. When all of the stamping is complete, fix the paint colour by pressing the fabric with a hot iron for 2–3 minutes.

TIP

If you choose different colours for this technique, make sure they will mix to make a third colour. Some ready-mix paints are not formulated to be mixed, and some colour combinations will yield only a muddy brown or gray.

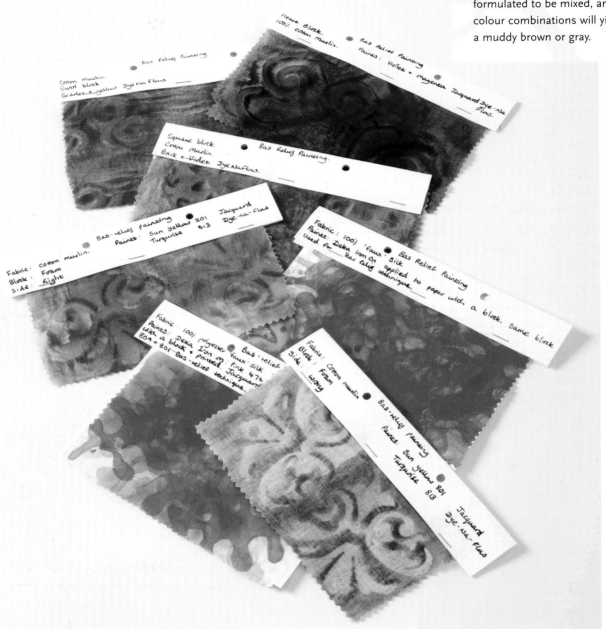

Air and heat from a blow-dryer pushes the paint into the fabric that is in the deeper areas of the printing block. These low areas will be dark in tone, leaving the fabric on the actual printing surface of the printing block a paler colour. The reverse of the fabric should have an even more striking contrast. The side you use is a personal choice.

Pot Colouring with Fabric Paints

All you need to do to colour silk or polyester faux silk is scrunch fabric in the bottom of a pot or mug and then sprinkle dye across the surface. This process is quick and easy, and gives great, although unpredictable, results.

Control the dye saturation in wet fabric by placing it in a container and then dripping dye onto it.

MATERIALS
* fabric
* fabric paint
* blow-dryer
* iron
* large paintbrush, plastic syringe or small pipette
* plastic pot or pint-size beer mug
* plastic sheeting

1. Spread a clean sheet of plastic sheeting over your work surface. Wet the fabric and scrunch it up in the bottom of a pot or mug. Using a large paintbrush, plastic syringe or small pipette, drip colour onto the fabric.

2. Lightly work the dye into the fabric with a large paintbrush, turning the fabric to make sure the colour reaches all parts. Do not saturate the fabric with colour.

The paintbrush is an ideal tool for working the dye into the fabric.

3. Lift the fabric out of the pot and place it on a clean sheet of the plastic-covered work surface, leaving it scrunched up. Place the fabric bundle in a warm location and leave it to dry. To hasten the process, you can dry the balled up fabric with a blow-dryer set on low so that the fabric is not disturbed. Iron the fabric for a couple of minutes to set the colour.

Drying the fabric in this way, while it is balled up, yields a random colour pattern. This effect is ideal for backgrounds for embroidery or garment linings.

This technique is so-named because you use a plastic pot for the dyeing. A plastic, pint-size beer mug is ideal for smaller projects, or an ice cream tub for holding more yardage. The lining fabric used for the Velvet Snood project on page 36 was dyed in this manner using Jacquard Dye-Na-Flow, but any silk paints will work well.

Colouring with Indigo Dye

Indigo is a technique for the more enthusiastic dyer, but it is important to know how to work with it because this blue is such an enduring fashion colour.

A stock solution is not difficult to make, although the chemicals used are hazardous if not handled carefully. The upside is that the stock will keep for years and will dye up to a meter of fabric at a time. Not everyone has the space to maintain a 10-gallon (50 L) indigo vat, so an alternative is to make a stock solution.

Indigo powder will not dissolve in water. It needs to be changed temporarily into a form that is soluble. This is done by making a stock solution of soluble indigo, which can then be added to as little as $1/2$ gallon ($2 1/2$ L) of water, which is about three quarters of a washing-up bowl or dishpan.

The soluble indigo stock needs to be kept free of oxygen, so it is important not to splash it about! The following process for colouring natural fibres came about by experimenting with an original recipe from Phyllis Baron and Dorothy Larcher, who were ground-breaking English textile dyers and printers in the 1920s and 1930s.

All of the specified chemicals can be obtained from the companies listed in Resources, page 124. Always use a nonbiological detergent such as Ecover, which does not have colour enhancers or softeners, to wash an indigo-dyed finished item, and always do a wash test on samples before starting a big project.

NOTE: Care must be taken when making the stock. A caustic soda solution will burn the skin. It is essential to wear a respirator because the fumes from sodium dithionite are hazardous.

Only natural fabrics will take up indigo dye.

Using protective goggles and gloves, mix the chemicals in the specific order listed in step 1.

Gently place wet fabric in a large plastic bowl so that as little oxygen as possible gets into the dye solution.

MATERIALS

* indigo dye, natural or synthetic
* sodium hydroxide (caustic soda)
* sodium dithionite (hydros)
* water
* 2-quart (2-liter) glass, ceramic or heavy-duty plastic container with lid

* nonbiological detergent, such as Ecover
* glass or plastic pipette
* plastic spoons
* protective goggles
* respirator
* rubber gloves

1. Wearing a respirator, protective goggles and rubber gloves, put the following ingredients (in the order listed) into a 2-quart (2-L) ceramic, glass or heavy-duty plastic container with lid, stirring all the time with a plastic spoon. (**NOTE:** Always add the caustic soda to the water, never add water to caustic soda.)

   3 ounces (85 g) of sodium hydroxide dissolved in
   28 ounces (0.83 L) of water

   3 ounces (85 g) of sodium dithionite (sometimes called hydros)

   8 ounces (225 g) indigo dye, natural or synthetic

2. Stir the solution thoroughly for a few minutes. A thick purplish scum will appear on the surface. Let the solution stand for 10 minutes.

3. Pour $1/2$ gallon (2 $1/2$ L) of 61°F (16°C) water into a large plastic bowl. Sprinkle $1/4$ teaspoon (1.2 g) of sodium dithionite into the water with a plastic spoon. Let this solution stand for 5 minutes. This removes excess oxygen from the water. For a dark blue colour, add 7$1/2$ tablespoons (110 ml) of the stock solution to the water and dithionite in the plastic bowl without splashing. A glass or plastic pipette is ideal for making the addition. For a medium blue colour, add 11$1/2$ teaspoons (55 ml) of stock; for a pale blue colour, add 5$1/2$ teaspoons (27 ml) of stock. Let the solution stand for half an hour.

4. Wet the fabric by soaking it in water with a little detergent (just a quick squirt from a squeeze bottle is enough). Gently lower the fabric into the large plastic bowl, taking care not to splash or create bubbles. Leave the fabric under the surface for 1 minute.

5. Very carefully pull the fabric over to the edge of the bowl. Lift the fabric from the indigo dye, squeezing the fabric gently on the side of the bowl so that the excess liquid runs down the sides without splashing.

6. Hang the dyed fabric outside and leave the yardage there for at least 6 hours. This allows the indigo to oxidize so that the colour develops. Do not worry if it rains; this will not remove the colour from the fabric.

7. Rinse the fabric in hot water and then wash it at 104°F (40°C) using a nonbiological detergent.

The quantities in the above recipe will dye about a yard (meter) of fabric. After that the dye will be exhausted, containing only water and sodium dithionite. To revive it, add a little water that is 61°F (16°C) to the vat to raise the temperature. Then sprinkle about a $1/4$ teaspoon (1.2 g) of sodium dithionite onto the surface of the liquid and wait for 5 minutes. Add more stock solution (see step 3), wait half an hour and proceed as before.

Soak the fabric in the indigo dye solution for a minute.

Carefully remove the fabric from the container, gently squeezing out the excess dye.

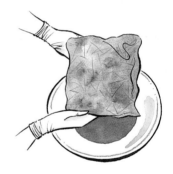

The fabric will look green as it comes out of the indigo but will turn a glorious indigo blue as it is exposed to the air.

TIP

If a fabric comes out paler than expected after completing step 5, try dipping it again for an additional minute. Try this before adding more stock, as some fabrics are more difficult to dye than others.

Dyeing with Walnut Ink

Walnut ink in the form of crystals or liquid is a very handy way of achieving a variety of coffee colours ranging from pale to dark. The resulting dye can be applied to fabric after mixing it with water. To improve the colour and fastness, the fabric needs to first be treated with a mordant, in this case alum (potassium aluminium sulphate or potash alum, which comes as a white crystal or powder). Alum is nontoxic, but it can irritate if it is inhaled. It is always sensible to wear a respirator when measuring chemicals of any kind, toxic or not.

The recipe that follows will treat approximately 2 yards (1.9 m) of cotton or linen. The dye works best on natural fabrics, preferably vegetable fibres. Walnut dye will not colour synthetic fabrics permanently and gives only very pale colours on silk, although some tussah dyes will work—do experiment.

See Resources, page 124, for a list of places to purchase alum and walnut crystals or ink.

Varying amounts of walnut crystals placed in 4 ounces (114 ml) of water will create a wide range of dye effects.

MATERIALS

* fabric
* alum
* hot water
* clothes dryer
* pan
* walnut crystals or ink

TIP

Start by adding 1 teaspoon (5 ml) of ink crystals to 4 ounces (114 ml) of water. Keep the amount of water consistent and add more crystals to make up different strengths.

1. Dissolve 7 ounces (200 g) of alum in about 8 ounces (220 ml) of hot water. Add this mixture to approximately 3 1/2 gallons (4 L) of warm water. Wet the fabric, place it in the mixture and leave it to rest for a few hours. Keep the temperature of the mixture at about 140°F (60°C) by topping up with hot water as needed.

2. Rinse the fabric thoroughly in hot water to remove any surplus alum, and spin it dry in a clothes dryer to remove as much surplus moisture as possible. Leave the fabric damp, to improve take-up of the walnut dye.

3. Make up a solution of walnut ink. Different fabrics take up the dye in different ways. Refer to the manufacturer's instructions to make ink with walnut crystals. Experiment to determine the amount of ink you will need. Place the ink in a pan and bring it to a boil. Add the fabric and simmer for half an hour. Remove the fabric from the pan and rinse it well in hot water. Walnut crystals will dye without heat but the results are very pale and most of the dye washes out.

NOTE: It is always advisable to keep dyeing utensils and kitchen utensils apart.

Different fabrics take up walnut dye in different ways. The deepest colours are obtained on brushed cotton. Mid-range colours show up on calico, linen and muslin. Very pale colours appear on silk. The colours stand up well to washing but, as with fabrics dyed with indigo, always use a nonbiological detergent and always do a wash test on samples before starting a big project.

This bag is made from fabric and trims dyed with walnut ink crystals. It matches the Corset Jacket on page 32.

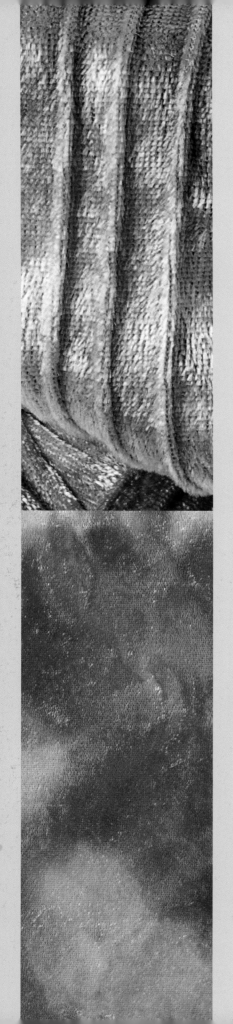

CHAPTER 2

Keeping it Simple: Creating Surfaces with Two Stitches

If you want to design individualized clothing and accessories but feel discouraged because you think your machine is too basic, don't be! Wonderful effects can be achieved using just two utility stitches that are included on all modern machines. With straight and zigzag stitches, the most unpromising fabric can be transformed into a feast of colour and texture. The zigzag stitch can be lengthened and narrowed until it almost looks like a curvy line, or shortened to produce a satin stitch. The six techniques shown in this chapter will yield base fabrics that can then be used for bags, hats, jackets and shoes. At the end of the chapter are three projects showing how you can use your skills to produce a jacket, a snood and a clutch bag.

Using Running and Zigzag Stitches

This technique gives you the opportunity to add both colour and texture to a base fabric. The technique is essentially the same in all cases, but simply varying the type and colour of thread, or first dyeing the base fabric, can have a dramatic effect on the results.

MATERIALS

* base fabric
* felt
* fusible webbing, such as Wunder-Under (Bondaweb)
* general purpose presser foot
* machine embroidery threads

1. Prepare the base fabric by colouring it, if desired.

2. If the fabric has a loose weave or is slippery enough that it needs to be stabilized, apply a backing to the wrong side. Felt is suitable. You can adhere it with fusible webbing. This will allow for even stitching.

3. Working from the top to the bottom of the fabric, make rows of stitching about a presser foot–width apart. Use a standard (all-purpose) presser foot. Experiment if desired.

4. Fill in the fabric with additional rows of stitching. Next, add varied stitching lines, possibly using different thread colours.

The sample shown in the photographs is cotton muslin that was first coloured with fabric paints using the bas relief method on page 17. The fabric was backed with felt before stitching. Cotton muslin needs to be stabilized in this manner because it has an open weave that can distort during stitching unless a firm backing is used.

The fabric was stitched with a metallic thread in the needle. For the same effect, you can use an all-purpose or bobbin thread in the bobbin, stitching from the top to the bottom of the fabric. I have then varied the stitching by adding lemon, and then lilac, viscose threads. Viscose threads such as Victory Embroidery Thread from the Thread Studio (see Resources on page 124) and Madeira are ideal for adding a bit of sheen to fabric.

TIP

Make a set of samples. On one, work all of the lines of stitching in the same direction, from the top to the bottom of the fabric. On the other sample, alternate the stitching direction: top to bottom and then bottom to top. Note any difference in the shape of the base fabric; some fabrics distort if the stitching is all in one direction.

Start by stitching a few lines up and down the fabric.

Build up the concentration of lines, looking at—and experimenting with—the way that the colours work with one another.

TECHNIQUE 8

Using a Twin Needle

Synthetic fabrics with a bit of stretch can be transformed by the addition of close, parallel rows of straight stitching performed with a twin needle.

All machines will stitch with a twin needle. Twin needles are constructed with two shafts on a crossbar that extends from a single shank. These needles are especially useful for heirloom and decorative stitching, and anywhere else that may require multiple, uniform rows. If your machine has only one spool holder, consider buying a spool stand (available from most machine suppliers), or try putting the spool into a container behind the machine, bringing the thread over the machine and threading it as usual. If you find that the threads tangle, make sure that the thread on the right spool feeds off the spool clockwise, goes through the right side of the tension disk and is threaded through the right needle. The thread from the left spool feeds off counterclockwise, through the left side of the tension disk, and through the left needle.

Some pattern stitches can be worked with a twin needle, but always turn the hand wheel manually through the entire stitch pattern to make sure that the needles clear the throat plate on both sides. A needle size of 3.0/90 is the largest needle with which you can make pattern stitches.

MATERIALS

* fabric
* decorative machine embroidery thread
* twin needle

1. Load the thread and test-stitch on a scrap of fabric. One bobbin thread feeds through all of the stitching. This results in a raised fabric tunnel on the right side, between the two parallel lines of straight stitching. Polyester velvet is a good choice for this technique. The stretchy nature of the velvet gives the tunnel effect without having to alter tension. It is especially important to do a sample before stitching the project.

2. Begin stitching with the twin needle, always working in the same direction, from the bottom of the fabric to the top, for example. With polyester velvet, always stitch at right angles to the stretch. Stitch without a backing because the stretch of the fabric is needed to produce the texture. Repeat this sample stitching alternately from top to bottom, then bottom to top. Note any differences, and use whichever method works for your chosen fabric.

3. Add multiple rows of straight stitching as desired.

NOTE: Sizing for twin and triple needles is slightly different than other specialty needles. Two numbers are listed on the packaging; the first number represents the distance between the needles and the second number is the European needle size. For example, a 1.6/80 double needle means that the needles are 1.6 mm apart and the shaft is an 80 European (12 American).

Polyester velvet, available in mouthwatering colours, looks especially sumptuous when decorated with rows of twin-needle stitching.

A 6.0/100 needle produces the most dramatic texture, as shown in this sample.

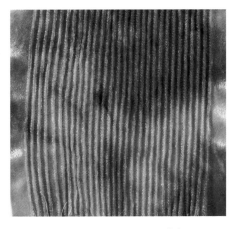

A 3.0/90 needle creates a more subtle texture.

Adding Motifs to Create Pattern

A combination of two fabric decoration techniques can produce an exciting background with a pattern.

TIP

Avoid spray-on fusible adhesives as they can mark fine fabrics. Try a fusible webbing, such as Wunder-Under (Bondaweb).

MATERIALS

* cotton muslin (a fine, open-weave fabric)
* lightweight fabric
* fabric paint
* printing block (stamp)
* fusible webbing, such as Wunder-Under (Bondaweb)

1. Use fabric paint and a printing block (stamp) to make a background pattern on cotton muslin.

2. Using the same printing block and paints, print designs on polyester silk or other lightweight fabric. Apply fusible webbing to the back.

3. Cut the motif shapes, without seam allowances, from the polyester silk.

4. Using fusible webbing, stabilize the back of the cotton muslin with felt. Place the motifs, right side up, on the right side of the cotton muslin. Iron the motifs to attach them to the cotton muslin.

5. With the fabrics right side up, sew multiple rows of straight and satin stitching over the surface.

In this sample, cotton muslin was bas relief painted (see page 17) with Jacquard Dye-Na-Flow fabric paint in brick and violet colours, using the heart printing block. The motifs were made from polyester silk using the same block and violet and pink transfer paints. These motifs have been cut out, attached with fusible webbing and stitched down into the background with tightly spaced rows of straight and satin stitch.

LEFT
The more stitching you can put onto these backgrounds, the better. The stitching emphasizes the background and blends in the overlaid motifs.

TECHNIQUE 10

Using Cable Stitches

This is a special way to machine stitch with thick threads that will not fit through the eye of a sewing machine needle. You stitch with the front of the work facedown, so that the bobbin thread ends up decorating the front of the work. The thick thread lies on the top of the fabric and the thinner top thread wraps it, anchoring it to the fabric, and shows only slightly.

This technique gives you the opportunity to work with some exciting thick threads that are often discounted. These can be used effectively if they are handwound onto the bobbin and the stitching is done on the back of the work.

TIP

As a general rule, use threads that are the thickness of perle cotton and avoid slubbed yarns. (These can be couched instead, as explained in Applying Strip and Sew Couching on page 30.)

MATERIALS
* fabric
* felt
* fusible webbing, such as Wunder-Under (Bondaweb)
* all-purpose thread
* decorative thread

1. If working on an unstable (loosely woven) fabric such as cotton muslin, use a fusible webbing to add a felt backing.

2. Start by making lines of medium-length straight stitches on the right side of the fabric with a machine embroidery thread to tone with the fabric. This will give you guidelines to follow when you stitch from the back. (**NOTE:** You will leave these stitches in the fabric so they become part of the finished effect.)

3. Wind the thick thread onto the bobbin. Handwind the thread if it has some stretch or your machine makes it difficult to feed the thread onto the bobbin.

4. Adjust the needle tension so that the bobbin thread is not pulled into the fabric.

5. With the wrong side of the fabric facing you, start stitching. Build up the lines until you have the effect that you want.

The sample shown at right has been worked on a background of cotton muslin backed with felt, with a thick, space-dyed thread handwound onto the bobbin. The shiny viscose threads are a decorative product created for over-locking (serging), called Madeira Décor. This is a good thread to start with as it will wind onto your bobbin and stitch without problems.

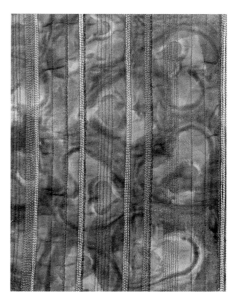

Cable stitching makes the most of thicker threads and results in a lovely, textured surface.

Applying Strip and Sew Couching

Couching attaches a narrow material to a backing fabric by employing zigzag stitches that work up the length while straddling both sides of the lacing, ribbon, or yarn.

You can expand on this basic technique by also using straight and satin stitching and including some less traditional materials.

MATERIALS

* dyed fabric
* fabric scraps
* decorative or all-purpose threads
* felt
* fusible webbing

1. Select and dye your background fabric. If necessary for a loosely woven material, stabilize by using a fusible webbing to secure felt to the back.

2. Select and prepare materials that will be applied to the backing. Lay them out in different combinations, varying texture for added interest. Torn strips of fabric are very effective. Scraps of lace can be painted with fabric paints to add texture.

3. Sew fabric strips to the backing at regular intervals, leaving gaps where the other materials will be applied. Use evenly spaced rows of straight stitching along the length of each fabric strip, leaving the raw edges free. Decorative thread can be used in the needle, bobbin or both positions.

4. Attach the remaining materials to the background fabric, one at a time, varying the order as desired. Use straight stitching along the center or one edge of a material, or zigzag stitching through or around it. Do not worry about making the stitching lines perfectly straight. Again, decorative or all-purpose thread can be used. It is not necessary to backstitch at the beginning and end of the stitching lines.

The two samples at right (top and middle) were worked on a background of brushed cotton that has been dyed with walnut ink, as explained on page 22. A piece of cotton muslin (a fine, open-weave fabric) was bas-relief dyed, as explained on page 17, with a leaf printing block (stamp) and pewter, violet, and yellow fabric paints. Scraps of lace were painted with violet. A matching viscose machine embroidery thread was used to work narrow strips of satin stitch. Two fine polyester voile fabrics were torn into strips, stitched down, and then burnt with a craft heat gun. This burning bonded the fabrics together. Space-dyed viscose chenille knitting yarn was crocheted into lengths of loosely worked cable stitches and then sewn to the fabric surface with a straight stitch.

TIP

Change the scale of the couching materials to match the project. The sample with narrow fabric strips below, top, would look good made up as a small bag. The larger sample below, middle, would make an attractive jacket panel.

Straight stitch fabric strips to the backing.

Layer other interesting materials between the fabric strips.

Try working on tapestry canvas as a background. This gives a strong base for items such as bags. If you stitch from the back, with the decorative thread in the bobbin, as explained in Using Cable Stitches on page 29, the canvas makes it easy to stitch in a straight line. These types of canvas can be painted with fabric paints and left visible as part of the design.

Making Layered Circles

This technique celebrates the diversity of complementary fabrics by letting bits of each show through interesting shapes that are created by overlapping satin-stitched circles.

A sample is necessary, as the response of each machine will be different. Some will stitch quite happily without a sewing hoop; some will need the fabric to be hooped.

MATERIALS

* fabrics
* embroidery scissors
* masking tape
* thumbtack

1. Decide the desired width across your finished circle. Divide this in half. Starting at the needle position under the presser foot on the sewing machine bed, measure this distance to the right of the presser foot. At this position, use masking tape to attach a thumbtack (upside down so that the prong is facing upward). The thumbtack will be at the center of the stitched circle.

2. Layer the fabrics, starting with a felt base. Fabrics that may stretch, such as cotton jersey, might perform better near the bottom of the layers.

3. Push the fabrics onto the secured thumbtack, with the felt on the bottom. Adjust the sewing machine for a satin stitch (short zigzag). When the machine stitches, the fabric travels in a circle.

4. Stitch several circles, overlapping them, and then cut back sections of fabric to reveal the fabric underneath. Leave the last layer uncut.

TIP

Use a sharp pair of embroidery scissors to cut away layers of fabric. Work slowly, as it is very easy to cut through too many of the layers by mistake.

The sample above has been worked with indigo-dyed fabrics that were coloured to different tones. There are four fabrics layered on a felt background. The silk shibori went down first, followed by a pale blue cotton and then a deep blue cotton jersey. On top is a medium blue cotton.

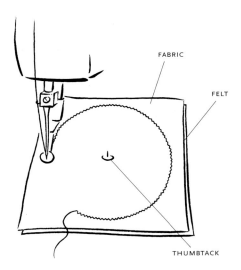

FABRIC

FELT

THUMBTACK

Some machines have an attachment that allows you to stitch in circles. Even a basic sewing machine, however, can achieve the same effect with a drawing pin, some masking tape and a backing such as felt. Depending on your machine and fabric, you may also need a machine-embroidery hoop.

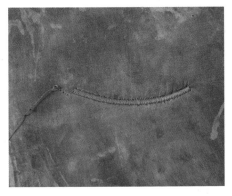

A thumbtack mounted on the bed of a sewing machine will make fabric layers travel in a circle. The circles may not always be perfectly round, which sometimes adds interest to a fabric.

Cotton, linen and silk were dyed with walnut ink before cutting and assembling the materials into this jacket with corset-shaped embellishment and busk fastening.

Corset Jacket

Corset styling adds artistic flare to a casual jacket. Adding to the overall effect, the front fastens with a traditional corset busk while the back features false lacing. The corset shape superimposed on the back and front is not a separate piece of fabric. It is created with embellishments and directional stitching.

The one-size jacket shown at left was made with natural fabrics dyed with walnut ink, as explained on page 22.

FINISHED SIZE

* 42" (105 cm) bust
* 21" (53.3 cm) center back length
* 16$^1/_4$" (40.6 cm) sleeve length (drop shoulder)

MATERIALS

* 3 yards (3 m) of 35"–36" (90 cm) -wide plain cotton or linen for base fabric

* 1 yard (1 m) of 34" (84 cm) -wide Thermogauze or vanishing muslin (a firm, brush-off, heat-dissolvable fabric)

* 3 yards (3 m) of 35"–36" (90 cm) -wide lining fabric

* approximately $^1/_2$ yard ($^1/_2$ m) each of 44"–45" (115 cm) -wide cotton, linen and silk, all dyed with walnut ink, for couching materials (see Applying Strip and Sew Couching, page 30)

* 2 yards (2 m) of 1" (2.5 cm) -wide (pressed width) bias tape made from fabric dyed with walnut ink (see Dyeing with Walnut Ink, page 22)

* 11" (28 cm) straight corset busk for the front closure

* all-purpose cotton, polyester cotton or polyester thread to match

* 1 yard (1 m) firm cord for back lacing (see Making Machine-Wrapped Cord, page 51)

* decorative machine embroidery thread such as YLI Machine Quilting 100% Long Staple Cotton, colour cream to brown, for attaching and defining the outline of the corset shape

* thick threads of various types for defining the corset shapes

* 1" (25 mm) bias tape maker (optional)

* baking parchment

* pattern paper

* pencil

* Corset Jacket Front, Back and Sleeve pattern pieces (see the patterns, page 114)

* Corset Shape pattern piece (see the pattern, page 115)

* awl

* eyelet kit, with small or medium eyelets

* tailor's chalk

1. Enlarge all the pattern pieces to full size and trace them onto pattern paper. Use them to cut out the fabric pieces from the base fabric and the lining as follows: Cut 1 back and 2 sleeves, all on the fabric fold. Cut 2 fronts. Seam allowances are already included in the pattern pieces.

2. Using a pencil, trace 4 corset shapes onto the Thermogauze. Transfer the diagonal stitching line from the corset shape to each Thermogauze shape. Cut out the shapes and set them aside.

3. Using the Strip and Sew Couching technique on page 30, apply strips of dyed and neutral fabric and a few lengths of trim vertically to the right side of all of the jacket fabric pieces.

4. Using tailor's chalk, trace the paper corset shape onto the right side of both front fabric pieces. Also trace the corset shape onto the right side of the back, leaving a gap at center back. Flip over the paper corset shape and trace the mirror image on the other side of the center back line (**A**). Set aside the paper corset shape. Within the corset tracing lines, place lengths of various threads, plus snippets of fabric and lace onto the front and the back fabric pieces.

5. Cover the right side of the back fabric piece with a Thermogauze corset shape. Pin it in place. Cover the opposite side of the back with another Thermogauze corset shape. With decorative sewing machine thread in the needle and bobbin, sew parallel rows of straight stitching through all of the layers, along the direction of the diagonal line on the pattern, using the machine's presser foot as a guide (**A**). Cover and stitch the fronts in the same manner.

6. You may like to outline the corset shapes by satin stitching or couching around the edges with a decorative thread such as YLI cotton. If desired, remove the Thermogauze now (with a hot dry iron) by following the rest of the instructions in this step, or delay the removal until step 13 is complete. Place the stitched pieces under baking parchment and press with a hot iron until the Thermogauze disappears. The snippets of thread will be trapped underneath the top stitching and the corset shape will be clearly seen on the pieces.

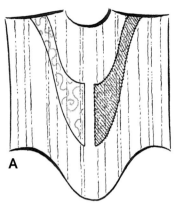

TRACE CORSET SHAPE ON FABRIC

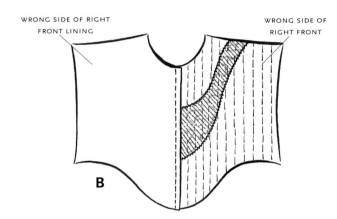

WRONG SIDE OF RIGHT FRONT LINING

WRONG SIDE OF RIGHT FRONT

B

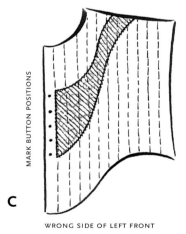

MARK BUTTON POSITIONS

C

WRONG SIDE OF LEFT FRONT

D

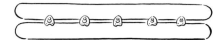

The busk fastening is two pieces. This will close the jacket at center front.

7. Attach the busk fastening to the front edges of the jacket and mark the openings for the loop catches onto the Jacket Front as follows: Place the loop side of the busk on the wrong side of the right front fabric piece, aligning it with the vertical front edge seam line ($^5/8$" [15 mm] from the raw fabric edge), between the top and bottom of the corset shape. Mark each loop position on the fabric. Remove the busk (**B**). With the right sides of the right front and lining together, sew the lining to the front edge of the Jacket Front with a $^5/8$" (15 mm) seam allowance, leaving gaps as marked for the busk loops.

8. Turn the lining to the inside of the jacket. Insert the busk. To prevent the busk from moving, topstitch it through all fabric layers, close to the long edge of the busk, the edge without loops (**B**).

9. Position the remaining half of the busk on the wrong side of the left front fabric piece. Shift the busk so that one long edge is $^7/8$" (22 mm) away from the vertical front edge. Mark the position of the busk buttons on the wrong side of the fabric (**C**). Remove the busk and pierce the fabric with an awl at each button position.

10. Make a row of eyelets just inside the straight vertical edge of both corset shapes in the back piece, using an eyelet kit and following the manufacturer's instructions. Thread the lacing cord through the eyelets (**D**).

11. Sew the lining to the left front with right sides together. Put the busk in place, pushing the buttons through the holes made in the fabric. Fold the lining to the inside of the jacket and stitch it in place close to the long, vertical edge of the busk.

12. Place the wrong sides of the back lining and back fabric pieces together with all raw edges matching. Sew all of the edges together with an overcast stitch. Use a straight, and then zigzag, stitching if your machine does not have an overcast stitch. Secure the lining to the remaining edges of the fronts in the same manner.

13. With the right sides together, stitch the binding to the bottom of the sleeve and turn the loose edge to the

wrong side. Hand- or machine-stitch the binding in place on the inside of the jacket. If desired, make 2 additional lines of straight stitching on the bias binding, through all layers with decorative thread in the needle.

14. Make up the jacket by stitching the pieces together with $^5/8$" (15 mm) seam allowances and using an overcast stitch or straight stitching followed by zigzag stitching. Stitch the shoulder seams first. Stitch the sleeves to each side of the jacket by matching the center of the top of the sleeve to the shoulder seam. Complete by stitching the front and back of the jacket and the sleeve underarm in one line of stitching.

15. Stitch bias tape to the bottom hem and top edge of the jacket as for the sleeves.

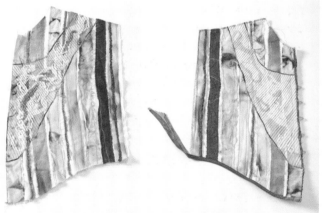

Turn lining to the inside of the left front along the seam line and then insert the busk buttons through the holes that were previously punched through the front fabric.

The jacket's raw edges are clean-finished by a simple application of 1" (25 mm) -wide bias tape.

Make the jacket in indigo dyed fabric, using pale, medium and dark tones.

Velvet Snood

Twin-needle stitching on stretch polyester velvet yields an elegant and versatile snood. Let it sit around your neck as a collar, or pull up the back to wear it as a hat.

The stitching could not be easier. After covering the velvet with rows of twin-needle stitching, it is attached to a lining and then the short ends are joined to make a tube. The finishing touch is another, smaller, twin needle—stitched tube that hides some of the seams.

Yardage for the pink and lilac snood, shown on page 39, was pot coloured with Dye-Na-Flow fabric paints (see Technique 4 on page 19). The blue and green snood, right, was made with yardage that was coloured by a manufacturer. Polyester velvet comes in many bright colours, so you do not need to paint your own fabric.

A twin needle and straight stitching is all you need to cover a stretchy velvet fabric with visual texture.

MATERIALS

* 1 yard (1 m) of stretchy polyester velvet for the outside (**NOTE:** Stretch velvet is usually 60" [150 cm] wide, although this varies from batch to batch. The width is not crucial, as you are stitching at right angles to the stretch, which is across the width of the fabric. In step 1, you need to cut a width and depth of 31" [79 cm] for the snood.)

* 1/2 yard (1/2 m) of 35"–36" (90 cm) -wide silk or lightweight polyester for the lining

* 6.0/100 twin needle

* 3.0/90 twin needle

* all-purpose polyester sewing thread

1. Cut out a 31" (79 cm) square of stretch polyester velvet (**A**).

2. Using the 6.0/100 twin needle (**B**) and starting about 3/4" (1.9 cm) from a raw edge, stitch from one side to another at a right angle to the stretch (**A**) and (**B**). Alternate the direction of the rows of stitching. In other words, work from top to bottom on the first row, bottom to top on the second, and so on. This stops any distortion. Use a standard (all-purpose) presser foot as a guide for spacing the rows.

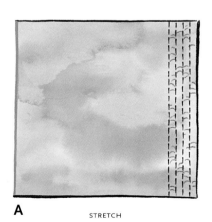

A   STRETCH

B

3. Continue stitching parallel rows until the entire piece is covered. When complete, it should measure approximately 18" x 29" (46 x 74 cm) (**C**).

4. Cut the lining fabric ¹/₂ " (12 mm) wider and ³/₄" (1.9 cm) longer than the stitched velvet. The longest side of the lining can be parallel to either the lengthways or crosswise grain line. Using the pot colouring technique on page 19), colour the yardage with fabric paints.

5. With the right sides of the fabrics together and using a ⁵/₈" (15 mm) seam allowance, stitch the lining to the lengthways edges of the velvet, with the long bottom edge of the lining being joined to matching bottom edge of the velvet, and the long top edge of the lining being joined to the matching top edge of the velvet (**D**).

6. Turn the joined pieces rightside out. Flatten the tube and baste together the raw edges of the lining and velvet at one short end. Baste the edges of the remaining raw edges in the same manner. Bring together the opposite, short, basted ends. Overlap the sides about ¹/₂ " (12 mm) and seam them together with an overcast stitch (use a straight stitch followed by a zigzag stitch if your machine does not have an overcast stitch). The fabric is now a tube, as shown (**E**).

7. Change the sewing machine to a 3.0/90 twin needle. Cut a new piece of matching stretch polyester velvet fabric approximately 8¹/₄" x 32" (21 x 82 cm). This fabric needs to be cut so that the stretch is across the width (**F**). This piece will cover the seam on the snood.

8. Starting about ³/₄" (1.9 cm) from one end, stitch seven sets of twin needle stitching lines parallel to the lengthways edge, spacing the sets about a presser foot width apart.

9. Place the stitched piece flat on the work surface. Measure the width across the stitched sets. Leave as much fabric again unstitched and trim any remaining fabric off the lengthways edge. Fold the partially stitched strip in half lengthways and with the right sides together. Sew into a tube using a ⁵/₈" (15 mm) seam allowance and straight stitching (**G**).

10. Turn the tube rightside out. Flatten it on the work surface so that the seam runs down one side of the tube.

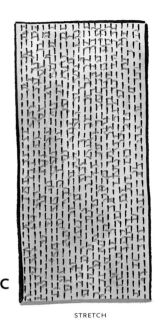

C

STRETCH

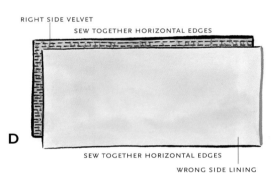

RIGHT SIDE VELVET

SEW TOGETHER HORIZONTAL EDGES

D

SEW TOGETHER HORIZONTAL EDGES

WRONG SIDE LINING

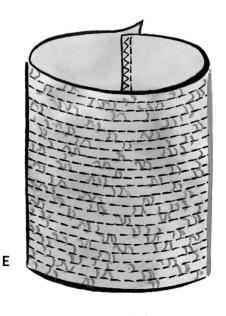

E

11. With the twin-needle stitching facing out, place the middle set along the seam line on the tube. Make sure that the top and bottom of the smaller tube extend above and below the snood. Pin both long edges of the each side of the tube and stitch it down, using the outer edge of the twin needle stitching as a guide (**H**).

12. Turn the snood inside out and hand-sew the tube down over the inner seam (**I**).

TIP

Check the exact measurement of the stitched piece of velvet before cutting out the lining. Different velvets will stitch up to different finished dimensions.

8 1/4" (21 cm)

32" (82 cm)

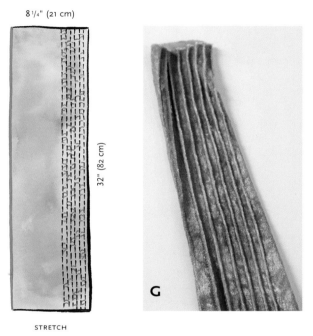

F

STRETCH

G

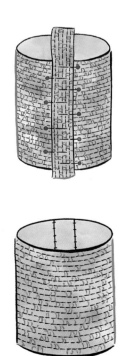

H

I

PROJECT 3

Simple Clutch Bag

Rich fabrics and threads are combined to produce a sumptuous surface that looks more complicated than it is. Only two stitches are used: running and satin. This simple clutch design is based on rectangles, and stitching on canvas is an easy way to keep a rectangle shape. Use the measurements given, or scale them up or down to produce your own unique version.

MATERIALS

* 3 pieces of tapestry canvas:
    * 1 piece 10" x 16" (26 x 40 cm) for the main body
    * 2 pieces 4$^1/_2$" x 2" (11.25 x 5 cm) for the gussets

* 1 piece of felt 11" x 17" (28 x 44 cm) for the inner lining of the main body (**NOTE:** This will be cut to size after it has been bonded to the lining fabric.)

* 3 pieces of lining fabric:
    * 1 piece 11" x 17" (28 x 44 cm) for the main body
    * 2 pieces 4$^1/_2$" x 2" (11.25 x 5 cm) for the gussets

* 1 yard (1 m) paper-backed fusible webbing such as Wunder-Under (Bondaweb)

* polyester thread to match

* machine embroidery threads

* 1 magnetic bag catch

* sharp craft knife

* small hammer

* selection of fabrics and laces for embellishment

* folding diagram (see page 43)

* pressing cloth

folding diagram (see page 43)

TIPS

Always use a polyester thread for the construction of accessories. Machine embroidery threads are spun with very little twist and are not strong enough to hold up to the wear and tear an accessory will endure.

Always use a lighter thread in the bobbin so that the stitching showing on the outside of the bag will blend into the fabric.

1. Stitch the strips of embellishment fabrics—all running in the same direction—to the three pieces of rug canvas, using the strip and sew couching technique (see page 30) (**A**). Experiment with the width of the fabric strips. The lace can go between, or on top of, the fabric strips. Make sure that the strips of fabric and trims extend past all edges of the rug canvas by at least $^{1}/_{2}$ " (12 mm).

2. Fold the fabric and trim edges to the back of the rug canvas and top stitch them in place (**B**).

3. Using the fusible webbing, bond the main body piece of the lining fabric to the corresponding felt piece. Always bond felt and lining together before cutting to size because the fabrics can stretch as they bond. Cut the bonded lining/felt fabric to 9 $^{1}/_{2}$ " x 15 $^{1}/_{2}$ " (24 x 40 cm) (**C**).

NOTE: Do not use a spray adhesive as it can mark delicate fabrics.

4. Only the main lining piece is bonded to felt. If the gusset linings are bonded to felt, they become too bulky to stitch neatly. Trim both of the gusset lining pieces so that they are just smaller than the gussets. Using fusible webbing, bond a lining piece to each of the rug canvas gusset pieces. Using a decorative thread and satin stitch, stitch across the top edges of the gusset pieces, to give a decorative edge. When the lining and the outer fabric of the bag are sewn together, the lining will be approximately $^{1}/_{4}$" (6 mm) smaller than the outer fabric.

5. To fasten the bag, attach both parts of the magnetic catch. Attach one part to the lining and one part to the outside of the bag (**D**). One part of the catch goes on the underside of the flap. The other part is on the outside of the bag so that the flap closes over it. On the outside of the main body of the bag, mark the position for the catch in the center of a shorter side of the embellished rug canvas and $1^{1}/_{2}$ " (3.75 cm) in from the edge. On the lining side of the lining/felt piece, mark the position the catch in the center of a shorter side of the fabric and 1" (2.5 cm) in from the edge.

NOTE: Check these measurements carefully before attaching the catch. Your clutch bag measurements may be different, so alter the positions of the catch parts if necessary.

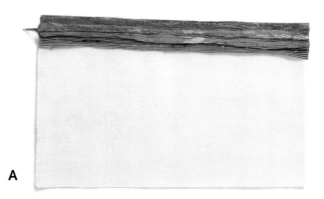

A

B

C

D

5" (12.5 CM)

FOLD LINE

1" (2.5 CM)   FOLD INWARD

BOTTOM

1" (2.5 CM)   FOLD LINE

5" (12.5 CM)

FOLD LINE

TOP FLAP

4" (10 CM)

E

FOLDING DIAGRAM

F

G

6. Attach a part of the magnetic catch by carefully cutting two small slits into the fabric with a sharp craft knife. Push the prongs on the catch through the fabric and secure the backing plate over the prongs. Use a small hammer to flatten the prongs against the backing plate. Attach the remaining part of the catch in the same manner.

7. Using a short, narrow zigzag (satin) stitch, sew around all edges of the bonded lining/felt piece. This is decorative stitching, because it will be seen on the inside of the bag.

8. Bond the lining/felt main body to the wrong side of the embellished rug canvas main body using fusible webbing. The lining/felt piece will be 1/2" (12 mm) smaller on all sides. Use a straight stitch, as close to the edges as possible, to attach the lining to the embellished canvas around all of the edges.

9. With a very hot iron and a damp pressing cloth, press the folds into the main body of the clutch bag. Follow the measurements shown on the folding diagram (**E**) above. When closed, there will be a bit of extra fabric at the upper edge, to create a top for the purse.

10. With a very hot iron and a damp pressing cloth, press the gusset pieces in half lengthways.

11. Attach the gussets to the main body. Stitch the bottom edges first. Attach one side of the gusset, and then the other (**F** and **G**).

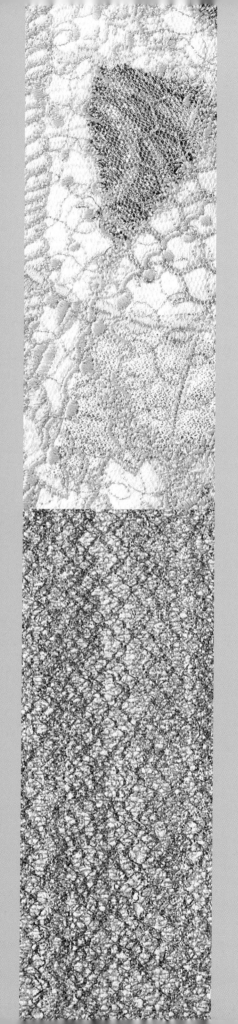

CHAPTER 3

STITCHES GALORE: WORKING WITH FREE-MOTION, UTILITY AND DECORATIVE EMBROIDERY

BASIC STITCHING IS ALL YOU NEED TO PRODUCE A RICHLY embroidered surface that is especially useful for decorating jackets and producing small items.

You will be amazed at just how much you can do even if you have a very basic sewing machine. Do play around with what you have; try combining stitches and patterns, layering them up or altering their sizes.

Embroiderers with sophisticated machines will have an array of stitches to play with. If you are in this situation, do not be confused by too many choices. Experiment with all of your options. You will soon find your favorite stitches and patterns and learn to be creative with them.

The first portion of this chapter explores six free-motion embroidery techniques. In all cases, you start with the feed dogs on the sewing machine in the down position, or covered if you have an old machine. The normal sewing foot is swapped for a darning foot. The final technique swaps the darning foot for the general-purpose presser foot and has the feed dogs up. The corset shown at right was stitched using this technique.

Whatever the technique, always loosen up by doodling on a scrap of fabric—it takes time to get the hang of free-motion embroidery. Doodling also allows you to check the tension of the stitching and verify that it is right for your project. Write your name, make shapes, even stitch on top of previous stitches.

Remember to be aware of your own tension. Try not to grip the fabric or hoop too tightly, and remember to breathe!

At the end of the chapter are four unique projects that show how basic and more complicated stitches can be used to create and decorate.

The lush surface of this corset is made by layering pattern stitching over felt, fabric snippets and tulle. See page 52 for more on this technique.

Embroidering with Free-Motion Running Stitches

This technique allows you to use the sewing machine in a very free and creative way. You are actually using the needle as you would a paintbrush. I encourage you to do lots of samples using different base fabrics and a variety of threads. Free-motion stitching enables you to develop an individual style.

MATERIALS

* base fabric
* printing block (stamp)
* fabric paint
* decorative machine embroidery thread
* paper-backed fusible webbing such as Wunder-Under (Bondaweb)
* darning presser foot
* embroidery hoop.

1. Choose a printing block (stamp) with a swirl design. Paint the base fabric and heat-set the motifs.

2. Lower the feed dogs (or cover them, as required for your machine), attach a darning presser foot and thread the machine as normal. Do not alter the tension at this stage. Put a test piece of fabric into an embroidery hoop. Place the hoop under the foot. Bring the bobbin thread up through the fabric and hold both top and bobbin thread with one hand while making the first few stitches. Stop the machine after a few stitches and cut away these loose threads.

3. Start to stitch. You will find that you can move the hoop in any direction. For even stitches, move the hoop slowly and run the machine quickly. If the hoop is moved too quickly—or with sudden jerks—the needle may break.

4. Take another piece of test fabric and use fusible webbing to back it with felt. Stitch as explained in the previous step, but without the hoop. Some stitchers like the security of a hoop, others prefer the freedom of fabric that is not in a hoop. Do whatever feels right for you.

5. Follow the outlines of the swirl design with free-motion stitching. Build up the layers of stitching.

TIPS

Move the fabric slowly while running the machine quickly. Imagine that you are a swan: serene above the water surface, paddling furiously underneath.

Cotton muslin is a fine fabric that distorts when stitched if not backed with another fabric. This sometimes gives a lovely textured effect, so experiment with different methods.

Start your free-motion project by doodling. Play around with letters and shapes. Try writing your name.

The sample shown above has been worked on a piece of cotton muslin (a fine, open-weave fabric) dyed with fabric paints using the bas relief painting technique (see page 17). The muslin has been backed with felt and stitched without a hoop.

Creating Free-Motion Zigzag Stitches and Satin-Stitch Beads

Free-motion zigzag stitching has a wonderful spontaneity. It lacks the perfection of normal zigzagging and gives an interesting line of stitching on a bas relief printed background, which is explained on page 17.

MATERIALS

* muslin
* felt for backing or embroidery frame (machine embroidery hoop)
* paper-backed fusible webbing such as Wunder-Under (Bondaweb)
* printing block (stamp) with a regular pattern
* decorative machine embroidery threads in several colours
* fabric paints
* darning presser foot

1. Paint the fabric using the bas relief technique (see page 17). Back the muslin with felt, using the fusible webbing.

2. Lower the feed dogs (or cover them, as required for your machine), attach a darning presser foot and thread the machine needle and bobbin as normal. Do not alter the tension at this stage. Switch to a medium-width zigzag stitch.

3. Place a fabric scrap in a hoop or use fusible webbing to attach felt to the back of the fabric. Stitch on the fabric scrap, experimenting with the machine settings. Again, you are in complete control. Move the fabric slowly and run the machine quickly. Make the zigzag stitches close together for satin stitch lines, and then apart for zigzag lines. If the work is moved too quickly—or with sudden jerks—the needle may break.

4. When you are comfortable with the stitching, switch to the project fabric. Make lines of satin stitching to outline the pattern of the block. Stitch several lines in different threads.

5. Stitch the beads on the tiny squares, alternating the colour of the needle thread. For each bead, keep the fabric in one place and let the stitches build up, one on top of the other. Move to another part of the fabric and stitch another bead. The joining bobbin and needle threads between the beads can be left on the fabric or cut away.

TIPS

Larger beads can be made with a rectangle of satin stitching in one colour, and then changing the thread colour, turning the work 90 degrees, and stitching another bead on top.

Some fabrics, especially fine ones, will need to be in a hoop. You can tell if a fabric needs a frame because it will be hard to control, and stitching will make it pucker. Thicker fabrics can be stitched without a hoop. Using paper-backed fusible webbing such as Wunder-Under (Bondaweb), you can attach a backing such as felt to a fine fabric, so that you do not need a hoop. Do stitch without a hoop if you can, as you will have more freedom to move the fabric around.

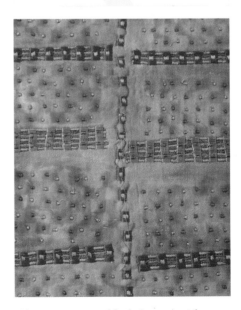

Choose a printing block (stamp) with a regular pattern for this technique. This sample was made with a block that has tiny squares. The zigzag stitch width was set at medium.

Filling with Vermicelli Stitches

This is a great fill stitch that is worth the time it takes to get it looking right! The squiggly stitching lines are named after the Italian pasta and translate as "little worms."

If the thought of stitching this pattern is too daunting, draw a pattern of squiggly lines on fabric with a fine indelible marker and then stitch over the lines.

MATERIALS

* base fabric
* felt for backing or embroidery frame (machine embroidery hoop)
* paper-backed fusible webbing such as Wunder-Under (Bondaweb)
* variegated machine embroidery thread
* darning presser foot
* fabric paint
* printing block (stamp)

1. Paint the fabric using a printing block (stamp) with a curved design that will give interesting areas to fill with vermicelli.

2. Set up the machine as for free-motion running stitches (see page 46) and back the fabric sample with felt (using a fusible webbing to join the pieces) or frame (hoop) the fabric.

3. Outline the design with free-motion running stitches.

4. Using a variegated machine embroidery thread, fill in areas of the design with vermicelli stitching as follows: Moving the fabric slowly while running the machine quickly, meander over the fabric in half circles. The half circles should stay as one line. Do not cross other lines of stitching.

Experiment with vermicelli stitching on different fabric backgrounds. Put your samples into a book. This stitching is worked on a layered background of satin and polyester voile, which was coloured with transfer paints. The "word" motif was cut from transfer-dyed nylon organza and applied with vermicelli stitching.

This example uses the negative space created when "word" was cut out of the transfer-dyed nylon organza. The vermicelli stitching secures the fabric to the underlying layers.

RIGHT

Illustrating how it can be used as fill, vermicelli stitching was worked on the same sample as free running stitch. The running stitches follow a swirl design.

Dyed silk and scrim are the layered background of this sample. Rows of automatic stitches were worked over vermicelli stitches in metallic copper, orange, pink, purple and yellow. The monogram is from a Victorian seal.

Loosening the Bobbin Thread for Whip Stitching

When stitched correctly, the top thread is completely covered by the bobbin thread and gives a lovely line of relief stitching on the surface of the right side of the fabric.

When making the stitch, the bobbin thread is pulled up and whipped around the top thread. The top and bobbin tension will need to be altered. Refer to the machine's manual for instructions on how to loosen the bobbin tension. It is a good idea to buy a second bobbin case just for this technique; this saves altering the tension each time you want to make whip stitching. The top tension needs to be set at 9, which, on most machines, is the tightest setting.

MATERIALS

* base fabric
* felt for backing or embroidery frame (machine embroidery hoop)
* decorative machine embroidery thread
* nylon monofilament thread such as YLI Wonder Invisible Thread 100 percent nylon (optional)
* additional bobbin
* darning presser foot

1. Back the fabric with felt or insert it in an embroidery hoop. Loosen the bobbin tension, adjust the machine's needle tension to 9 (the tightest setting) and lower the feed dogs (cover them on an older machine). Do not adjust the stitch length. As with all other free-motion techniques, the stitch width is determined by how quickly you move the embroidery under the needle: slowly for small even stitches, quickly for large stitches.

3. Thread the bobbin. Remember that the bobbin thread is the one that will be seen so use a decorative thread.

4. Thread a strong thread through the needle. Nylon monofilament works well, but experiment with whatever you have. This thread should not show, as the bobbin thread whips up around it.

5. With the right side of the fabric facing you, bring the bobbin thread up through the fabric and hold both top and bobbin thread with one hand while making the first few stitches. Stop the machine after a few stitches and cut away these loose threads.

6. Start to stitch, moving the fabric slowly and running the machine quickly. The bobbin thread will whip around the top thread and lie on the surface of the fabric. The top thread should be completely covered by the bobbin thread.

TIPS

When altering bobbin tension, always hold the bobbin case over a container. If the screw pops out, it won't be lost because it will fall into the container.

The thread needs to be free running from the bobbin case. Always loosen the bobbin screw a quarter turn at a time.

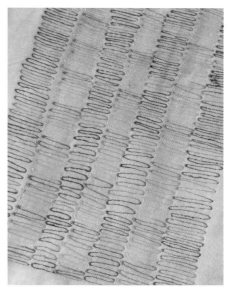

The sample has been worked on cotton muslin (a fine, open-weave fabric) that was first dyed with fabric paints using the bas relief technique (see page 17). The bobbin was loaded with a space-dyed machine embroidery thread, the top with a nylon monofilament.

Embellishing with Granite Stitches

Like vermicelli stitching, the granite stitch is a good filler. It is worked by stitching tiny circles, one on top of the other. The machine is set as for free-motion running stitch. Variegated thread looks great, but do experiment with single colours.

MATERIALS

* base fabric
* felt for backing or embroidery frame (machine embroidery hoop)
* variegated or plain machine embroidery thread
* darning presser foot

1. Paint the fabric, back it with felt and frame it, if preferred.

2. Thread the machine with a variegated machine embroidery thread in the bobbin and the needle.

3. Bring the bobbin thread up through the fabric and hold both top and bobbin thread with one hand while making the first few stitches. Stop the machine after a few stitches and cut away these loose threads.

4. Stitch in tiny circles, overlapping some of them. Experiment with the size of the circles, making them as tiny as possible and then larger, to approximately $1/8$" (3 mm). Always make a record of your samples.

TIP

Always remember that you are in control of the stitching when working free-motion embroidery. You are drawing with thread and will develop your own style. Do not try to copy my or anyone else's stitching. Do your own thing!

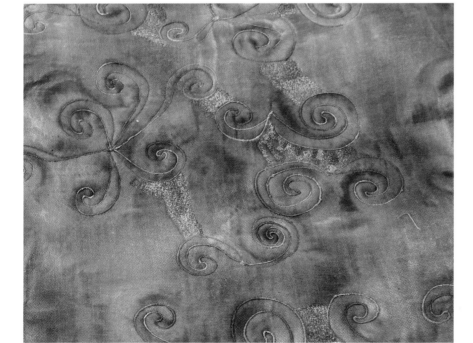

The sample shown at left has granite stitch worked in the spaces between lines of whip stitching (explained on page 49).

Making Machine-Wrapped Cord

A machine-wrapped cord is easy to produce and has so many uses. Use finished cord to edge jackets, make jewellery and make unusual fastenings for handmade books.

Your options for creating the cord are just as diverse. Choose interesting threads. Try metallic thread in the bobbin and variegated or space-dyed thread in the needle. It is possible to make soft or stiff cords by changing the core (filler) of the cord. Experiment with string, fabric strips, knitting wool, round elastic, stranded hand embroidery threads . . . anything!

MATERIALS

* core material such as knitting wool
* machine embroidery thread
* darning presser foot

1. Set the machine as for free-motion zigzag stitches (see step 2, page 47), making sure that the stitch is wide enough to cover the cord.

2. Hold one end of the core and the bobbin and needle threads in one hand behind the darning presser foot. Position the opposite end of the core in the other hand in front of the foot. Start to stitch over the part of the core lying under the presser foot. Sew slowly until you get the feel for the stitching. The bobbin and needle threads will wrap around the cord. At this point, make sure that your zigzag stitch is wide enough to go to either side of the core material and not through it.

3. Move the core slowly backward and forward until it is covered by thread. The top thread will be the most prominent, with the bobbin thread showing just a little bit.

TIP

Experiment with different thread textures. A matte top thread and a shiny or glitzy bobbin thread give interesting results.

A medium worsted-weight (chunky in the UK) yarn is an ideal core material for machine-wrapped cord. It was used for all of the samples shown at left.

Stitching a Fabric Collage

Layer upon layer of pattern stitching builds a lush surface worthy of any one-of-a-kind artistic garment. Stitches and strips or snippets of sheer fabrics can be combined on a plain fabric base to produce a firmly stitched surface that is suitable for belts, handbags, and jacket panels.

The step-by-step photos, right, show the materials used to create the corset shown on page 45.

MATERIALS

* felt, firmly woven cotton or other natural-coloured fabric for base fabric

* snippets of coloured fabrics

* tulle net (optional)

* paper-backed fusible webbing such as Wunder-Under (Bondaweb)

* decorative machine embroidery thread matched to the most often used dominant colours of the fabric snippets

* general-purpose presser foot, with the machine's feed dogs in the upper position

1. Start with a piece of felt, firmly woven cotton or similar neutral-coloured fabric. Cut some snippets of coloured fabrics.

2. Using fusible webbing, attach the fabric snippets to the base fabric.

3. Extra interest can be added by using small strips of tulle net over the fabric.

4. Using running stitch, zigzag stitch and any other stitches the machine has to offer, stitch over the snippets of fabric, matching the needle threads to the colour of the fabrics underneath.

5. These instructions are for samples, but experimentation is really important. Make other fabric samples, altering the length and width of the stitches for them.

Fuse random fabric shapes on a plain base, in this case metallic and silk fabrics on felt. Overlay the entire yardage with net.

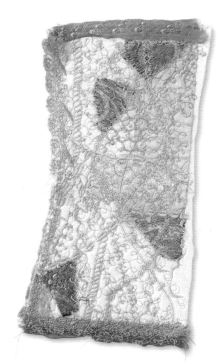

Pattern stitching through all layers holds everything in position. Two different needle threads were used: gold rayon showcases the pattern stitches while straight stitching was worked in a gold metallic.

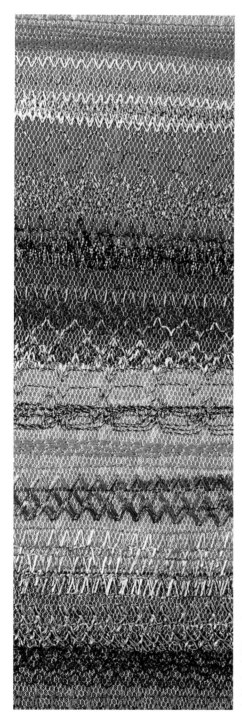

Strips of sheer fabric have been bonded to a tightly woven cotton and then stitches were worked over the top. The tension was kept at a normal setting, but the length and width of some of the stitches were altered. Sample worked by Barbara Taylor on a Bernina 1090.

Pattern stitches have been worked directly onto the fabric. Sample worked by Barbara Taylor on a Bernina 1090.

This heavily worked sample by Barbara Taylor was inspired by the landscape at Inch Strand in southwest Ireland. Strips of sheer fabrics were placed on a tightly woven cotton. Utility and pattern stitches combined to produce a rich surface.

Cord and Bead Necklace

You can make one-of-a-kind fabric necklaces to coordinate with any outfit. This is an excellent opportunity to try out the fabric bead techniques and machine-wrapped cord on pages 51 and 98, respectively.

MATERIALS

* 4 3/8 yards (4 m) of machine-wrapped cord
* sheer, 100 percent synthetic fabric for beads and finishing the ends of cord
* all-purpose thread, colour-matched to the sheer fabric
* darning/embroidery presser foot
* 3 push pins
* straight pins
* 6" x 15" (15 x 38 cm) mounting board such as Styrofoam
* masking tape or 2 bulldog (binder, clamp-style) paper clips
* heat gun

1. Make as many fabric beads as desired. Also make one larger bead.

2. Cut the stitched cord into three equal lengths. Thread each length with fabric beads.

3. Pin the three lengths together at one end and use push pins to attach them to a board. Braid the strands together, spacing the beads as desired (**A**).

4. Secure the top and bottom of the braid with tape or a paper clip and then remove the braid from the board. Thread the six ends of the cords through a large fabric bead and slide it up about 4" (10 cm).

5. Using all-purpose thread, sew a strip of fabric to the end of each cord with a few machine stitches.

6. Working on one cord end at a time, roll the fabric around the end and then use the heat gun to melt the fabric into a bead (**B**).

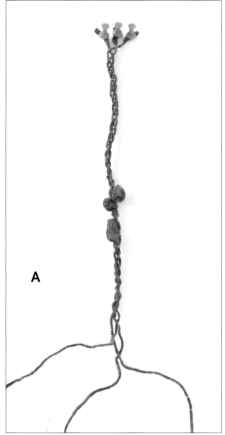

A

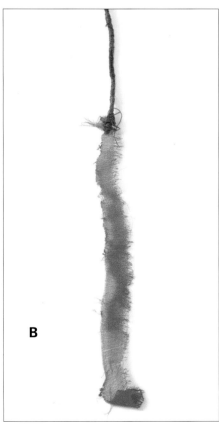

B

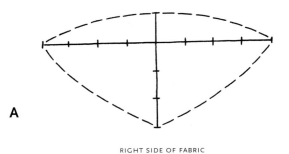

RIGHT SIDE OF FABRIC

PROJECT 5
Swirl-Painted Wrap

Using painted cotton muslin (a fine, open-weave fabric) and free-motion embroidery stitches, make a wrap for day or evening. The wrap shown opposite was painted using the bas relief technique (see page 17), but any painting technique could be used to colour the fabric. Parts of the fabric have been cut away and embroidery worked in the spaces. You could experiment with other embroidery techniques such as Applying Strip and Sew Couching on page 30.

MATERIALS
* 2¹/₄ yards (2 m) of 58"–60" (150 cm) -wide bas relief painted cotton muslin (a fine, open-weave fabric) or commercially printed fine fabric (Note: The fabric must be fine enough to drape over the body.)
* machine embroidery threads such as YLI Cotton (03V) in Madras
* ¹/₂ yard (¹/₂ m) of 34" (84 cm) -wide Thermogauze or vanishing muslin (a firm, brush-off, heat-dissolvable fabric)
* baking parchment
* darning presser foot
* sharp scissors
* straight pins

1. Fold the fabric in half across the width and length and mark the center point. Open up the fabric. Using the knuckles of your hand, measure four knuckles to the right, four to the left, one to the back, and three to the front, marking the outside edge of the last knuckle measurement in each direction. Create an oval neck opening by joining up the points and then cutting away the interior fabric (**A**). If you are making an item for a child, use the child's knuckles. This method of measuring the neck opening works for adults and children and will give an exact fit.

2. Find the center point of the neck opening at the front and cut the front opening, following the design of the fabric. This will give the wrap curved front edges.

3. Cut around the outside edge of the fabric, again following the design to give the wrap curved edges.

B

C

4. Using sharp scissors, cut away some shapes between the printed motifs (negative spaces) in the fabric design.

5. Pin pieces of Thermogauze to the fabric, behind each cut-out shape.

6. Set up the sewing machine for free-motion running stitches (see step 2, page 46). Even though cotton muslin is a very fine fabric, Thermogauze gives it enough weight to be stitched without a hoop or felt backing.

7. Stitch around the outside of each shape using granite stitch (see page 50). Remove the pins and stitch across the shape with free-motion running stitches, making sure that the stitching lines overlap in places, to lock them together (**B**).

8. Pin strips of Thermogauze to the edge of the wrap. Using granite stitch, stitch all around the edges of the wrap (**C**). Dissolve the Thermogauze with a hot, dry iron and baking parchment (see page 70).

Fun Day Jacket

This project allows you to have some time with your feet up, knitting squares. Your yarn is indigo-dyed fabric that has been cut into strips. The squares are sewn together to make a box-shaped jacket that is decorated with sewing machine pattern stitches.

FINISHED SIZE

* 40" (100 cm) bust
* 20" (50 cm) center back length
* 10" (25 cm) sleeve length (drop shoulder)

MATERIALS

* Dark-, medium- and light-colour indigo-dyed, medium-weight cotton such as pillowcase cotton for knitting:
    * $5^1/_2$ yards (5 m) each of 35"–36" (90 cm) wide of each value (dark, medium and light), or
    * $4^3/_8$ yards (4 m) each of 44"–45" (115 cm) wide of each value
* 3" (7.5 cm) squares of indigo-dyed natural fabric such as cotton, linen or silk, approximately 30 light and 30 dark
* colour-matched machine embroidery thread such as Gutterman Machine Quilting Thread in colours 5826 and 5624
* $7^1/_8$ yards ($6^1/_2$ m) of machine-wrapped cord (see page 51)
* heat-away, paper-backed fusible webbing such as Wunder-Under (Bondaweb)
* 3 buttons, each 1" (2.5 cm) wide
* quilter's gridded ruler, rotary cutter and self-healing mat or dressmaking scissors
* size US 11 (8 mm) knitting needles
* large, dull-point tapestry needle
* assembly diagram (see page 61)

1. Dye the cotton fabric with indigo (see page 20).

2. Cut each of the knitting fabrics into squares that are as large as the fabric width. For example, if the fabric is 35" (89 cm) wide, cut each square 35" (89 cm) wide and 35" (89 cm) long. This is very important as the fabric needs to be cut into strips on the bias. This will give the fabric enough elasticity to allow it to be knitted.

3. Fold each square in half diagonally. Cut the square in half along the diagonal line. Each square is now two triangles.

4. Using a rotary cutter, ruler and mat—or scissors—and starting at the longest edge, cut the fabric into strips, each one approximately 3/4" (1.9 cm) wide. Do not make the strips any narrower, as they will break under the tension of the knitting. Test a strip by pulling it hard to make sure that it doesn't break. The strip should stretch a little and the edge might fray slightly.

5. Tie the ends of the strips together to make one long length, mixing the long and short strips. This will avoid too many knots in one place on the reverse of the knitting. Roll the length up into a ball.

6. Each knitted square needs to measure 10" (25 cm). On knitting needles, using 3/4" (1.9 cm) -wide strips, you will need to cast on 30 stitches and work 40 rows of stockinette stitch (knit right-side rows, purl wrong-side rows). It is important to test the tension and adjust the number of stitches if necessary. The type of fabric used and the size of the cut strips will affect the size of the square. Position all of the fabric knots on either the right or wrong side of the knitting (**A**).

7. Knit 12 squares. Sew together the squares as shown in the assembly diagram, opposite (**B**). Use the measurement guide in step 1 of the Swirl-Painted Wrap (see page 56) to determine the size of the neck opening. Stitch the squares together using fabric strips threaded onto a large tapestry needle. Do not seam at the neck and front openings.

8. Decide which side of the knitting to use. The knotted ends will show on the reverse of the fabric.

A

9. Attach the small squares of fabric on the front of the jacket with fusible webbing. Attach squares on the underside of the fabric in the same places to prevent knitted fabric from catching in the feed dogs on the sewing machine.

10. Machine embroider on the squares with a pattern stitch. The finished jacket on page 58 features a wavy line that echoes the shape of a knit stitch. Sew strips of fabric to the edges of each square and tie the ends together.

11. Stitch around the outer edges of the jacket with a pattern stitch. You may need to stitch around the edge two or three times. As you stitch, stretch the fabric to produce a wavy edge. When stitching around the edge of the fabric, the stretching seems to stop any knitted loops from snagging in the presser foot.

12. Using the free-motion zigzag stitch (see page 47), attach the cord to all of the edges of the jacket, making three loops for the buttons along the right front edge as you go.

13. Sew buttons on the left front, opposite the button loops.

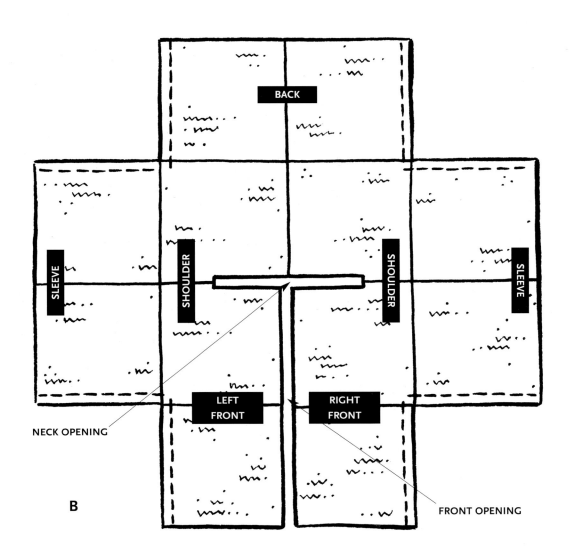

Money Belt

For times when carrying a handbag is inconvenient, this belt is also a purse that is large enough for a bit of cash, credit cards and even a slim cell phone. The belt is fastened with anorak poppers (heavy-duty snaps) that are spaced so that the belt will fit sizes 8 through 14 (UK 10–16). Machine embroidery motifs around the poppers form part of the decoration.

The idea for this project came from a belt made in Indonesia twenty-five years ago. Unfortunately, the original designer and maker are unknown. The original was adapted slightly to make it more comfortable to wear.

MATERIALS

* ³/₈ yard (¹/₄ m) of 44"–45" (115 cm) -wide cream-coloured, medium-weight fabric such as silk noil (raw silk)

* machine embroidery threads:

    * YLI Machine Quilting Thread colour 06V for the base of the Front Panel

    * Victory Embroidery Thread colours 1094 and 114 for the middle layer of the Front Panel

    * Madeira Rayon 30 wt. colour 2004 for the top layer of the Front Panel

* 3¹/₄ yards (3 m) of machine-wrapped cord (see page 51) (**NOTE:** The machine-wrapped cord used for the money belt shown opposite has a core of knitting wool and is wrapped with Madeira Rayon colour 2004.)

* 4 anorak poppers (heavy-duty snaps)

* 8 small decorations stitched on Thermogauze (see page 46)

* 8" x 12" (20 x 30 cm) piece of heat-away, paper-backed fusible webbing such as Wunder-Under (Bondaweb)

* baking parchment

* dressmaker's chalk or pencil

* Money Belt Lining, Front Panel and Front Strap pattern pieces (see pages 115–116)

TIP

Always stitch fabric before cutting out a pattern piece because the fabric might become smaller after stitching. The 8" x 12" (20 x 30 cm) piece for the belt Front Panel will shrink to 6" x 10" (15 x 25 cm) when stitched.

1. Cut a piece of fabric 8" x 12" (20 x 30 cm). This piece will be stitched heavily with pattern stitches to form the Front Panel of the belt.

2. Using machine embroidery threads and a stitch pattern of your choice, embellish the fabric (**A**).

3. Enlarge the pattern pieces for the belt. Cut out 1 Front Panel from the stitched fabric and 2 from plain fabric. Also from the unstitched fabric, cut out 2 Front Panels, 2 Front Straps and 1 Lining (on the fold).

4. Using the fusible webbing, attach a plain fabric Front Panel to the back of the stitched Front Panel. With the right sides together, sew a Front Strap to each side of the stitched Front Panel.

5. Start to make the pocket in the lining by placing a plain fabric Front Panel facedown on the right side of the center of the Lining. Pin it in place.

6. Using chalk or a pencil, mark an opening on the Lining and stitch around this line, forming a narrow rectangle of stitching. Cut through the center and up into the corners. Remove the pins and turn the attached Front Panel to the inside of Lining through the opening. Press.

7. Stitch around the opening on the right side of the Lining, through all of the layers.

8. With the wrong sides together, pin the Front Panel to the Lining. Using the YLI thread and a decorative stitch, stitch the front and back pieces together around the edges, removing the pins as you stitch (**B**).

9. Build up the stitches around the edges with the different colours of thread, ending with the Madeira Rayon colour 2004.

10. Attach the machine-wrapped cord over the seam line that joins the embellished Front Panel to the Front Straps with a free-motion zigzag stitch set to a width that is slightly wider than medium.

11. Place a decorative trim on the right side of Front Straps at each popper position. Attach the poppers as shown in the instructions supplied with the kit, placing them on the marks indicated on the pattern. The top of the poppers go on the left strap of the belt; the bottom of the poppers go on the right side. The trims go between the fabric and each popper.

A

B

OPPOSITE
A commercially printed fabric was used to create this money belt.

CHAPTER 4

DISAPPEARING ACT: CREATING WITH DISSOLVABLE FABRIC AND UNUSUAL MATERIALS

INTRICATE TEXTURED SURFACES CAN BE CREATED BY THE use of dissolvable fabrics and machine embroidery. Dissolvable fabrics are available in two types: water-soluble and heat-soluble. There are many brands on the market. It would be advisable for you to try as many types as you can and find the ones that are best suited to your style of work. The dissolvable fabrics used in this chapter are my favorites. You may discover others.

Water-soluble fabrics are dissolved in either cold or hot water. Heat-soluble fabrics are the vanishing muslins and Kunin felts. How to use these four types are shown, step-by-step, with projects at the end of the chapter. One is a particular favorite of mine. It uses metallic candy wrappers and hot-water soluble fabric to create textured, metallic-looking nuggets that can be applied to a fabric base.

The corset at right is made from kunin felt and free-motion embroidery. See page 71 for more on this technique.

The images at left illustrate the process of making Juliet's lace. See page 68 for full instructions.

Creating Juliet's Lace

There are many types of cold water–soluble fabrics. Some look like clear plastic, others are more like a thin fabric. I find the clear plastic type the most useful. Aquatics Romeo Soluble Film is one of the best for making lace motifs. It is a heavyweight, water-soluble product, and can be stitched on without the use of an embroidery hoop. Romeo will even go through an ink-jet printer if you use a carrier sheet. Romeo is more difficult to remove than some of the lighter-weight water solubles, but this property can be really useful when making bags or belts where a bit of stiffness is required.

MATERIALS

* cold water–soluble fabric such as Aquatics Romeo Soluble Film
* decorative machine embroidery thread
* indelible, fine-tip permanent marker
* container of tepid water
* hot water

1. Trace your chosen design onto the Romeo with a permanent marker.

2. Using a close satin stitch, outline the design. The design can also be outlined in free-motion running stitch, working around the outline several times, to create a substantial edge for the design.

3. Fill in the main elements of the design with free-motion running stitch, crossing the lines of stitching over each other so that the stitching is locked together when the Romeo is dissolved.

4. Dissolve the cold water–soluble fabric by placing the work in a container of tepid water.

5. Keep changing the water until the Romeo has disappeared and you are satisfied with the amount of stiffness left in the stitching.

Build up a stitched design with a satin-stitched outline and overlapping free-motion running stitches. Once the Romeo soluble fabric is dissolved in cold water, you are left with a delicate lacelike motif.

Shirring with Hot Water–Soluble Fabric

Hot water–soluble fabric is invaluable for creating surface texture on light materials. The soluble fabric has to be boiled to be removed completely, but shrinking it at a lower temperature gives very exciting results. To avoid a disaster, it is best to use a thermometer to check the water temperature.

MATERIALS

* hot water–soluble fabric

* very fine chiffon such as the material in a chiffon scarf

* decorative machine embroidery thread

* fine, lightweight fabric, dyed and stenciled with acrylic paint
  (**NOTE:** Any type of acrylic paint will work.)

1. Place a piece of fine fabric on top of the hot water–soluble fabric.

2. Cover the silk with a piece of chiffon.

3. Using free-motion embroidery, stitch through all of the fabric layers, following the motifs, and then join the motifs with more open free-motion running stitches.

4. Boil a kettle of water and let it stand until the temperature is 167°F –176°F (75°C–80°C).

5. Pour the water over the stitched fabric. The hot water–soluble fabric will shrink, pulling the fabric in with it.

TIP

Measure the shrinkage using this technique. This will help you to estimate quantities for projects.

Never use water that is hotter than 176°F (80°C). If you do, the hot water–soluble fabric will disappear and the texture will be lost. The fabric sample at the top was exposed to 194°F (90°C) water, whereas the fabric at the bottom was dissolved in 176°F (80°C) water.

Start with a fine fabric that has been dyed and stamped. This silk was dyed with Jacquard Dye-Na-Flow, and the motif was stenciled with acrylic paint.

Place hot water–soluble fabric on the bottom and sheer chiffon on top.

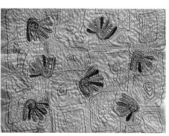

Free-motion motifs and running stitches bring the surface to life.

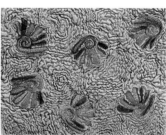

Hot water partially dissolves the soluble fabric while drawing in all of the layers.

Using Heat-Soluble Thermogauze Fabric

TIPS

Thermogauze can be used in single- or double-thickness. Use double-thickness when attaching an edge, such as on the shoes.

Never use a heat gun to dissolve Thermogauze—acrid fumes are produced.

Thermogauze is a type of vanishing muslin. It has the advantage of having a longer shelf life than other vanishing muslins. It is easily disintegrated by using a hot iron over baking parchment. This is particularly useful for edges and inserts, as Thermogauze disappears so easily. It is best used when a soft finish is needed, as there is no residue after the product is disintegrated.

The samples for the following steps show how to edge the shoe tops that are featured in the Summer Shoes project (see page 91).

MATERIALS

* vanishing muslin such as Thermogauze (a firm, brush-off, heat-dissolvable fabric)
* decorative thread that will not melt
* quilt pins with glass heads
* baking parchment
* iron

1. Pin a double thickness of Thermogauze to the edge of the fabric. Sew along the fabric edge using a decorative stitch or an ordinary overcast stitch. The overcast stitches look very good when stitched on top of one another.

2. Continue to build up the stitches by sewing on top of the previous stitches several more times, until you are satisfied with the results.

3. Cover the stitching with baking parchment and press the layers with a hot, dry iron for a few minutes. The Thermogauze will disintegrate leaving behind the decorative stitching. At first, the Thermogauze will turn brown. Rub it gently in your hands to dissolve and flake off, leaving the machine stitching visible and intact.

BELOW, LEFT
It is easy to edge the top of the Summer Shoes using Thermogauze. Simply pin a double layer on top, and then sew along the edge with an overcast stitch and decorative thread.

BELOW, RIGHT
The final step is heating the edge with a hot, dry iron and baking parchment to remove the Thermogauze.

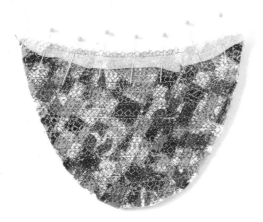

Working with Kunin Felt

Kunin felt is an acrylic and polyester blend available in many colours. A characteristic of some of the Kunin felts is that they can be dissolved by heating them with a heat gun. However, not all of the colours react in this way, so you will need to test your choice before using it in a project. The samples shown (below, right) were made with the denim blue colour. Make sure that you use Kunin felt, as other brands do not always work in this way. The dissolving process combined with stitching produces a delicate-looking yet incredibly strong lacelike fabric that is perfect for accessories.

MATERIALS

* Kunin felt

* Gutterman Machine Quilting Thread or Valdani Cotton Thread
  (**NOTE:** Some rayon threads will work, but most lose their colour before the felt has dissolved. Test your thread to make sure that it will not melt.)

* printing block (stamp)

* acrylic paint (**NOTE:** Any type of acrylic paint will work.)

* heat gun

* respirator

* wooden skewer or old paintbrush

1. Hold a heat gun over a scrap of your Kunin felt to make sure it will dissolve. Make sure the felt is on a heat-resistant surface. Cut a piece of felt large enough to allow for shrinkage. Using a printing block (stamp) and white acrylic paint, stamp a design onto the felt.

2. Using free-motion machine embroidery, stitch the printed motifs and then randomly embellish the surrounding fabric with additional stitching. Overlap some of the stitching lines when stitching around the motifs. Make the stitching very dense in some places and loose in other places. The random stitching lines should overlap, but this is not as crucial as it is with other dissolvable fabrics.

3. Using a heat gun, wearing a respirator and holding the gun approximately 2" (5 cm) from the felt, melt away the felt, leaving behind a lacelike fabric. Use a wooden skewer or the end of an old paintbrush to secure one corner of the felt while using the gun.

Densely stitched motifs come to life when stitched on Kunin felt that is later melted away. Start by creating your design on the felt. Next, stitch the surface (right, top). Finally, use intense heat to make the unstitched felt dissolve (right, bottom).

TIPS

Always wear a respirator when dissolving fabric with a heat gun, and work in a well-ventilated environment. Burning materials in this way can sometimes produce toxic fumes. Don't take risks with your health.

Dissolve the felt from the back—as well as the front—of the stitching. You can control the amount that the felt melts.

Creating Nuggets Using Metallic Candy Wrappers

Metallic sweet (candy) wrappers can be used very effectively with machine embroidery to introduce a glitzy element into stitching. Ferrero Rochers chocolates, in particular, are very useful for this technique as the wrappers are a lovely gold colour. The gold can be removed, if necessary, to give an antique effect. (See the tip below, right.)

When using sweet wrappers in this way, you are making slips, which are turned into stitched motifs or pieces that can then be applied to a base fabric. Use sweet wrappers together with soluble fabrics.

The stitched slips look a lot like gold nuggets.

MATERIALS

* any square metallic sweet wrappers such as Ferrero Rochers or a larger wrapper from a chocolate bar

* snippets of metallic thread, sequin waste and bits of glitzy fabric for the filler mid-layer

* hot water–soluble fabric, cut into squares the same size as the sweet wrapper

* very fine black chiffon such as the material in a chiffon scarf, cut into small squares 1" (2.5 cm) larger than the sweet wrappers

* decorative metallic machine embroidery thread such as Madeira Metallic FS 2/2 (also known as Madeira Metallic No. 20 Art FS 981)

* plastic bowl and hot water

1. Layer up the materials, starting with a square of hot water–soluble fabric on the bottom, followed by a candy wrapper. For the middle layer, add snippets of thread, fabrics and other items as desired. Place a square of chiffon on top of everything. Don't add too much embellishment to the middle layer or the wrapper won't shrink. Experiment to find out what works best.

2. Using free-motion running stitch embroidery, stitch around the outside edge of the square approximately ¹/₄" (6 mm) from the edge two or three times. This will help the layers remain square when shrunk. Stitch over the surface of the rest of the square with a few lines of stitching. The lines can cross over one another. Don't stitch too densely or the wrapper will not shrink. You really have to experiment to find just the right amount of stitching. It is not a problem if the wrapper tears.

3. Heat water to 167°F (75°C). Place the stitched piece in a plastic bowl and pour the hot water over the piece. The hot water–soluble fabric will shrink and produce a nugget.

TIPS

If you want an antique look, pour boiling water over the paper (right- or wrong-side-up) before layering it up in step 1. The gold will be partly removed.

A second technique produces a flat motif with a metallic base. The steps are exactly the same as for the instructions for using Romeo (see page 68), placing a metallic sweet wrapper under the Romeo after the motif has been stitched. Attach the wrapper with a few lines of stitching. This technique was used to make the Glitzy Belt (see page 81).

Experiment with different colours of cellophane sweet wrappers. I've used a red cellophane sweet wrapper over a gold metallic wrapper to produce a delicate pink nugget. Place the coloured cellophane sweet wrapper over a gold wrapper, then add the middle and upper layers. Place a sheer fabric on top.

Metallic candy wrappers covered with red cellophane were used to create a trim for this pink-and-gold bag. Rich Indian fabrics make up the base fabric, and the surface was created using techniques presented in Chapter 2.

T-Shape Soft Bag

TIPS

Always use a fine, lightweight fabric for this technique. It will draw up more attractively than a heavy fabric.

Stitch the fabric before cutting out the handbag pattern, as the shrinkage is impossible to judge accurately.

A charming little handbag is a great addition to any outfit, particularly when it repeats the motif or the fabric. The unique surface is sure to be a conversation starter. This project uses hot water–soluble fabric and free-motion machine embroidery to alter the surface texture of hand-dyed or commercially printed fabric. The finished fabric is then used to make this simple bag, which is named for the inverted T-shaped side seams that define its construction.

MATERIALS

* 1/2 yard (1/2 m) of 35"–36" (90 cm) lightweight fabric for the base fabric and the embellished fabric (**NOTE:** The samples shown in the photographs on page 76 were made with polyester silk that was dyed with Jacquard Dye-Na-Flow using the pot colouring technique [see page 19] and then printed with a design.)

* very fine chiffon such as the material in a chiffon scarf, in a colour that blends with the colour of the base fabric

* 3/8 yard (1/4 m) of hot water–soluble fabric

* 3/8 yard (1/4 m) of 58"–60" (150 cm) -wide felt

* 3/8 yard (1/4 m) of paper-backed fusible webbing such as Wunder-Under (Bondaweb)

* 1/2 yard (1/2 m) of thick cord for the core of the bag handles

* machine embroidery thread such as Valdani Cotton Thread

* 1 magnetic bag catch

* 4 small studs for the base of the bag

* double-sided sticky tape

* masking tape

* all-purpose polyester thread, colour-matched to the base fabric

* stiletto or sharp point for piercing the base of the bag

* thick card stock for 1 base board

* small hammer

* sharp craft knife

* T-Shape Soft Bag Body, Base, Base Board, Facing, Handle, Handle Lining and Body Lining pattern pieces (see pages 117–118)

1. You will need two pieces of embroidered fabric for the Body of the bag, each measuring at least 10" (25 cm) square (**A**). To make these, follow the step-by-step instructions for using hot water-soluble fabric (see Creating Juliet's Lace on page 68).

2. Enlarge all the pattern pieces to full size. Use them to cut out the fabric pieces from the base fabric as follows:

Embroidered fabric: 2 Bodies, 2 Facings

Felt: 2 Bodies, 1 Base

Fusible fabric: 1 Base

Unstitched fine fabric (for the base fabric): 1 Base, 1 Body Lining

Thick card stock: 1 Base Board

NOTE: The pattern pieces already include seam allowances. Set aside unstitched fine fabric and felt to cut out for the handles in a later step.

3. Using fusible fabric, bond felt to the underside of both of the embroidered Body fabric pieces. Bond felt to the underside of the Base that you cut from unstitched fine fabric.

4. Using the polyester sewing thread and a ³/₈" (1 cm) seam allowance, stitch a Body to each long edge of the Base fabric piece. Press the seam allowances toward the Base and topstitch them to the base (**B**).

5. Attach an embroidered Facing to both top edges of the Body Lining, with a ³/₈" (1 cm) seam allowance. Press and topstitch the seam allowances toward the Facings (**C**).

6. To fasten the bag, attach both parts of the magnetic catch. Both parts are attached to the embellished fabric facings, inside the bag, at the top. Attach a part of the magnetic catch by carefully cutting two small slits into the fabric with a sharp craft knife. Push the prongs on the catch through the fabric and secure the backing plate over the prongs. Use a small hammer to flatten the prongs against the backing plate. Attach the remaining part of the catch in the same manner.

A

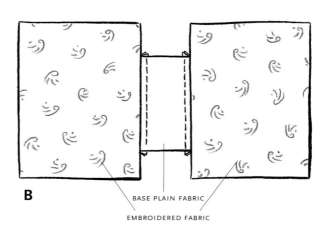

B   BASE PLAIN FABRIC

EMBROIDERED FABRIC

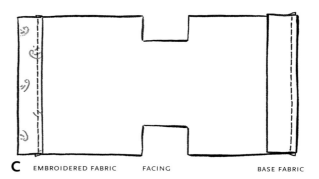

C   EMBROIDERED FABRIC   FACING   BASE FABRIC

7. With right sides facing, stitch the side seams of the embroidered fabric Bodies together with a $3/8$" (1 cm) seam allowance and press them open (**D**).

8. With right sides together, flatten the bottom of a joined side against the right side of the adjacent Base and stitch the Base with a $1/4$" (6 mm) seam allowance. Repeat at the opposite side.

9. Stitch the side seams and the base of the Body Lining as in steps 7 and 8.

10. Fix the Base card stock piece inside the bag with double-sided sticky tape. On the outside of the Base, mark the position for the four studs. Pierce these spots with a stiletto and insert the studs through the Base and the card stock. On the inside of the bag, open out and flatten the prongs of the studs. Cover the prongs with masking tape.

11. Dye and embellish plain fabric with stitched motifs, for the handles. Cut out 2 Handle pattern pieces from this fabric. Cut 2 Handle Lining pieces from felt. Using fusible fabric, bond a felt piece to the underside of both Handle fabric pieces.

12. Turn in every edge of the fabric Handles $3/8$" (1 cm) and press. Place a cord down the center of each Handle. Fold each Handle in half lengthwise and topstitch the folded edges together.

13. Position the Handles approximately 2" (5 cm) from the side seams on each side of the body, with the Handles flat against the sides and the Handle seams closest to the side seams. Stitch the Handles in place (**E**).

14. For both the Body Lining and the embroidered Body, turn under $3/8$" (1 cm) around the top edge and tack into place.

15. Drop the Body Lining into the bag. Pin the Body Lining and the bag together around the top edge, inserting the pins vertically. Topstitch the Body Lining and the bag together as pinned, sewing very slowly over the pins. Remove the pins.

TIP

Positioning the handle seams closest to the side seams ensures that when the bag is carried, the soft part of the bag handle is in the palm of the hand. This is more comfortable.

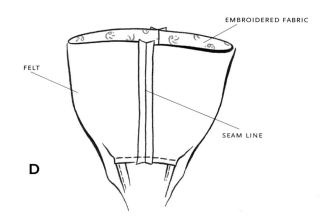

D

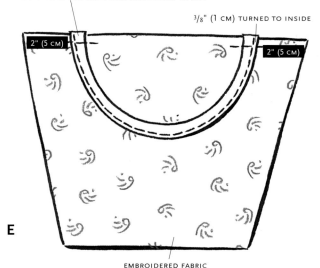

E

Hat in Kunin Felt

These lacy hats look delicate but they will stand up to harsh treatment and will squash into a suitcase. Stitch a lacy hat in Kunin felt for any occasion. Use trims such as stitched flowers to jazz them up. The hat comprises three pieces of stitched felt and is easy to make.

TIP

The hat can be permanently stretched slightly by stuffing it tightly with paper and leaving it overnight.

FINISHED SIZE

* The pattern will fit a head circumference of a medium adult (22" [56 cm]). Adjust the pattern pieces for a larger or smaller size as needed.

MATERIALS

* ³/₄ yard (³/₄ m) of Kunin felt 35"–36" (90 cm) wide. (**NOTE:** The hats featured at right and opposite were made with soft beige and denim blue.)

* decorative cotton machine embroidery thread that does not melt such as YLI Machine Quilting Thread or Valdani

* acrylic paint (Note: Any type of acrylic paint will work.)

* all-purpose sewing thread colour-matched to the felt

* heat gun

* printing block (stamp)

* respirator

* Hat in Kunin Felt Crown, Brim and Side Band pattern pieces (see page 119) (**NOTE:** Shrinkage allowance has been made in the pattern sizing.)

1. Enlarge all the pattern pieces to full size and cut them from the Kunin felt: 1 Crown, 1 Side Band and 1 Brim.

2. Using acrylic paint and a printing block, apply the design to the Kunin felt. Let the fabric dry.

3. Using a satin stitch (close zigzag) and decorative thread, sew around the outer edges of the pattern pieces. This stops the felt from shrinking too much when heated.

4. Using free-motion embroidery and decorative thread, stitch the main motifs and join them together with a free-motion running stitch.

5. Using a heat gun and wearing a respirator, dissolve the felt.

ABOVE
This hat has been stitched on beige Kunin felt with Valdani Cotton Thread, colour Glorious Fall number M62.

OPPOSITE
This delicate-looking hat was created using free-motion embroidery amd Valdani variegated thread on denim blue Kunin felt.

6. Measure the length of the Side Band and mark it off in quarters. Along the length of the Side Band, make two pleats so that this fabric piece measures 3" (7.5 cm) deep. Stitch across the fabric width to sew the pleats down at the 3 points that mark the quarter sections (**A**). Butt the short ends of the Side Band together and join them with a zigzag stitch, making sure that the stitch is wide enough to join the two pieces together. This gives a really neat finish.

7. Mark the center front and back of the Crown. Butt the edges of the pieces together and attach the Crown to the Side Band with zigzag stitching.

8. Butt the edges of the short ends of the Brim together and stitch this back seam with a zigzag stitch. Match the center front of the Brim to the center front of the Side Band and the center back of the Brim to the center back of the Side Band. Attach the brim to the Side Band with a zigzag stitch (**B**).

9. Fold the front of the Brim up to the Side Band and stitch it into place.

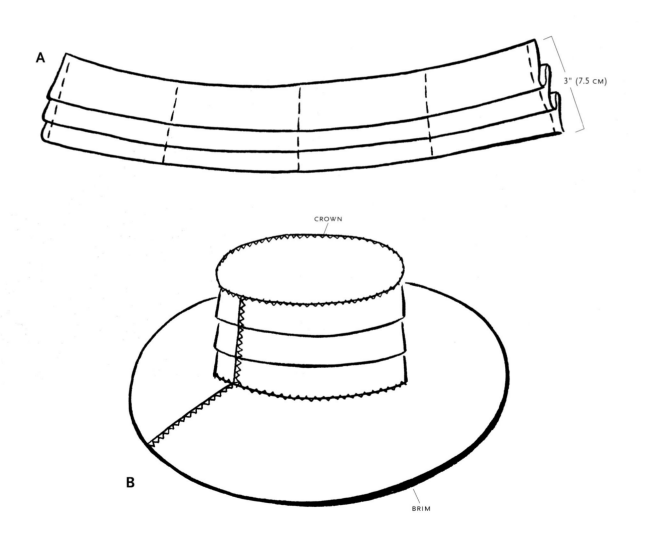

A

3" (7.5 CM)

CROWN

B

BRIM

Glitzy Belt

Who would guess that the most important material in this gorgeous belt is metallic sweet (candy) wrappers? This belt would be lovely for evening, worn against a black dress. The belt is flexible, yet has a bit of body from the use of the metallic paper and the cold-water soluble fabric. The belt is fastened with a concealed magnet that is encased in a waterproof membrane.

TIP

It's always a good idea to use magnets encased in a waterproof membrane for belts and jackets. If the item needs to be washed, the magnet will remain dry and won't rust.

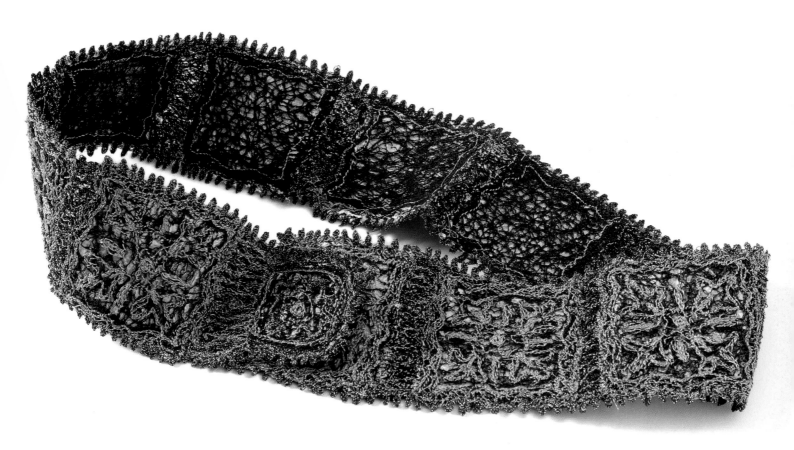

MATERIALS

* 20 metallic candy (sweet) wrappers measuring 3¹/₂" (9 cm) square
* 4 pieces of water-soluble fabric such as Aquatics Romeo Water Soluble Film, each one 4³/₄" x 40" (12 x 100 cm)
* decorative machine embroidery thread: black, gold and a black/gold twist such as Madeira Metallic (also known as Madeira Metallic No. 20 Art FS 981)
* sew-in magnet encased in a waterproof membrane
* fine-tip, permanent marker
* Glitzy Belt Motif and Catch templates (see page 120)

NOTE: For a size 10 (UK 12) belt, you will need 20 squares. Adjust the number of squares for a larger or smaller size.

1. Using a permanent marker, trace the design of the Motif onto a length of the Romeo 10 times, leaving a ³/₄" (1.9 cm) gap between each Motif. Trace the Catch Motif onto the right side of the row of motifs.

2. Put a second layer of Romeo under this layer and, using black thread in the bobbin and the needle, stitch around the perimeter of each Motif, using free-motion running stitches.

3. Stitch across each Motif in a grid (making sure that the stitching lines overlap) and then across the spaces in between each Motif.

4. Change to the gold thread in the spool and outline the main elements of the design in each Motif.

5. Attach a sweet wrapper to the underside of each Motif with a few lines of stitching around the perimeter and a bit in the center. Tear away the surplus sweet wrapper.

6. Draw the two outer (main) lines of Motifs on the second piece of Romeo, spacing them as explained in step 1. Place another layer of Romeo underneath this one. The second layer provides extra body while stitching. Stitch as before, but in black thread only. This will be the inside of the belt.

7. Attach a sweet wrapper as explained in step 5, tearing away the surplus.

8. Place both pieces of Romeo wrong sides together, making sure that the squares match up.

9. Using the black/gold twist thread, stitch around each Motif and across the gaps between Motifs with free-motion embroidery. Do not sew around the last Motif at each short end yet.

10. Sandwich one half of the magnet closure between the top and bottom Motifs for the last square on the right end of the belt. Stitch around the magnet, through all layers. Stitch the end squares together around the edges.

11. Stitch the other magnet inside the Catch Motif and stitch around the Motif.

12. Using the black/gold thread and free-motion embroidery, stitch a border all around the outside of the belt.

13. Place the belt in tepid water to dissolve the Romeo. Change the water until the belt is the stiffness you require.

*Glitzy motifs for the belts
are made using candy wrappers,
water-soluble fabric and
machine stitching.*

CHAPTER 5

New from Old:
Recycling with Style

ANOTHER TITLE FOR THIS CHAPTER COULD BE LARGE from Small, because all of the instructions illustrate techniques where small pieces of fabric are stitched together to form a larger piece. The fabrics that you start with can be either recycled or brand new, depending on the look desired.

There are two step-by-step techniques: One makes a new fabric from old lace; the second makes a larger fabric from small pieces of new fabric. Then you can learn how to apply your new knowledge to create a pair of charming summer shoes. For inspiration, you can examine the Victorian Corset shown at right.

The delicate-looking Victorian Miss corset, at right, was created by sandwiching lace between chiffon and a base fabric and stitching over the layers. The base fabric for this corset was designed by the author's grandfather and woven in Lancashire with the last Sea Island cotton to come into Britain after the start of World War II.

Using Vintage Lace with Chiffon

This technique was inspired by a quantity of old lace inherited from a grandmother, who had been a dressmaker. The bag contained small scraps—some really exquisite—but none large enough with which to do anything. There was also the problem of some of them being very old and fragile.

There are two ways that old (or even new) lace can be used to create a fabric.

MATERIALS

* neutral-colour, medium-weight base fabric such as a white cotton fabric dyed with walnut ink (**NOTE:** Lightweight fabric will work, but it must be a firm weave)

* lace snippets

* very fine chiffon such as the material in a chiffon scarf

* paper-backed fusible webbing such as Wunder-Under (Bondaweb)

* machine embroidery thread, colour-matched to the base fabric (**NOTE:** The neutral collection of Victory Embroidery Thread from The Thread Studio is just right for this technique. See Resources on page 124.)

* sharp, precise scissors

* straight pins

1. Using paper-backed fusible webbing, fuse pieces of old lace to the base fabric. Overlap the edges, position the pieces with spaces in between or layer them as desired to create a collage effect.

2. Cover the joined lace and base fabric with chiffon. Pin together the outer edges of the base fabric and chiffon.

3. Using free-motion embroidery (see the vermicelli and granite stitch techniques explained on pages 48 and 50, respectively) and machine embroidery thread, work into some of the motifs. The chiffon and fusible webbing secure the vintage lace pieces, so it is not necessary to cover the entire surface with free-motion machine embroidery.

4. This is an optional step. Using sharp scissors, cut away the chiffon that extends beyond the outer edges of the fabric and lace snippets that have been stitched down to the base.

Small lace pieces are fused to a cotton base fabric and then covered with cream-coloured chiffon. The base fabric was dyed with walnut ink.

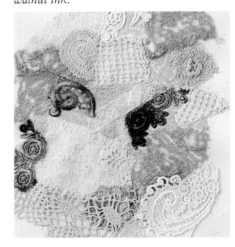

Granite stitch fills in spaces between lace tidbits, catching only the edges of some pieces.

TIP

The machine embroidery thread can be natural or synthetic, decorative or plain. You have flexibility because the chiffon overlay prevents harsher threads from damaging the precious lace snippets.

TECHNIQUE 26

Making New Heirloom Lace

Another way to work with lace, whether it is new or vintage, is to use Aquatics Romeo Soluble Film as a base and then link the pieces with free-motion embroidery. This method is useful if you need to preserve the lace quality of the pieces and want a fine, delicate effect without a base fabric. Romeo can be removed in cold water, so there is no danger to the fabrics.

MATERIALS

* lace snippets

* thick water-soluble film such as Aquatics Romeo Soluble Film

* machine embroidery thread matched to the overall colour of the lace pieces (**NOTE:** The neutral collection of Victory Embroidery Thread from The Thread Studio is just right for this technique. See Resources on page 124.)

* bowl of tepid water

* straight pins

1. Sandwich scraps of old lace between two pieces of Romeo. Overlap the edges, position the pieces with spaces in between or layer them as desired to create a collage effect. Pin the layers as needed to secure the edges and the position of the lace pieces.

2. Using free-motion running stitch (see page 46) and machine embroidery threads in the bobbin and needle, sew through the layers of Romeo, catching most of the edges of the lace pieces, to link the pieces together. Make sure that the stitching lines cross over one another.

3. Dissolve the Romeo from the lace and stitching by placing the work in tepid water. Soak the piece for 10 minutes, rinse, soak for a further 10 minutes and rinse again. Continue soaking and rinsing as needed.

TIP

Lace pieces can be fine or quite heavy for the techniques in this chapter. Quite heavy pieces produce a lovely textured surface when contrasted with fine stitching. The combination is really your design decision.

The base fabric does not need to be the same colour as the lace pieces. This is a personal choice. The lace pieces, however, should be in the same colour range and tonality.

TIP

Change the water frequently so that every bit of Romeo is removed. It can sometimes take several hours to completely dissolve the film, but it is worth the wait.

A firm, water-soluble film is a great base for stitching together precious lace snippets.

After the Romeo soluble film is dissolved, you are left with a large, delicate lace collage. The work shown above also includes a piece of embroidered lace net.

Piecing with Patchwork

This is a great technique if you have small pieces of precious fabric that are too small to use on their own. Like lace, bits of material can also be joined to create a larger fabric. The samples shown in the photographs for this technique at right are fabrics from The India Shop (see Resources, page 124). These fabrics, which are sold as patchwork pieces, come in lovely colours such as black, brick, cream, and denim blue.

MATERIALS

* 9 or 12 squares of fabric, each approximately 4" (10 cm) square

* 20" (¹/₂ m) square piece of lightweight, tightly woven fabric, for the base

* removable backing such as Pellon Stitch and Tear (**NOTE:** The backing does not have to be removed but does give a firm base to the fabric squares and makes cutting easy.)

* paper-backed fusible webbing such as Wunder-Under (Bondaweb)

* decorative or plain machine embroidery thread that blends with the fabrics

1. Arrange the fabrics, side-by-side, in a square on top of the removable backing. If you want to create a larger piece, overlap the edges of one or more pieces of removable backing. Try not to place the same fabrics next to each other. Do not overlap the fabrics. Butt the edges up against each other.

2. Stitch the pieces into place by sewing together all of the edges with a zigzag stitch.

3. Cut each row of squares in half, rearrange the cut sections and then stitch the edges together as explained in steps 1 and 2.

4. Turn the piece 90 degrees and cut the rows in half. Rearrange the new pieces and stitch them together.

5. Repeat steps 3 and 4 until you have ¹/₂" (12 mm) squares. Using a paper-backed fusible webbing, bond the stitched squares onto a backing fabric. Sew over the whole surface with a pattern or utility stitch.

Special fabrics take on a new purpose when joined together on a backing. Try to combine some light squares with others that have medium tones, and still others that have dark tones. It is best to stick with three colours.

You do not need to add a new piece of Stitch and Tear each time the cut pieces are reassembled. One layer is usually firm enough to make it possible to butt the pieces together and join them, but this will depend on the capabilities of your sewing machine.

This piece was stitched with a rayon embroidery thread and an overcast stitch, which can be found on most sewing machines.

The number of fabric squares that you will need depends on the desired finished size of the piece. It is most important that the shapes are squares, not rectangles.

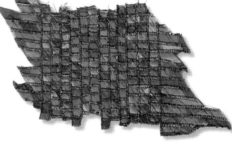

LEFT
This soft bag was made up using pieced fabric heavily embellished with a pattern stitch.

These fabric shoes are ideal for the beach but are strong enough to wear every day. You could experiment with different fabrics for the uppers. This pair is made with plain fabrics, but you could try glitzy fabrics and beads for a really individual look.

Summer Shoes

Richly embellished shoes don't require a fancy kit or top-of-the-line, heavy-duty sewing machine. These casual shoes are ideal for the lazy days of summer. The soles are rubber so they will stand up to a lot of wear and tear.

You can stitch these simple summer shoes from pieced patchwork, as explained on page 88.

FINISHED SIZES

* Small: Size 3–4, with a sole length of $9^3/4$" (25 cm)

* Medium: Size 5–6, with a sole length of $10^3/4$" (26.5 cm)

* Large: Size 7–8, with a sole length of 11" (28 cm)

MATERIALS

* 15" (38 cm) square of Piecing with Patchwork fabric for the Upper (see page 88)

* 15" (38 cm) square of plain medium-weight, tightly woven lining fabric for the sole

* paper-backed fusible webbing such as Wunder-Under (Bondaweb)

* piece of thin wadding (cotton or polyester batting) 8" x $10^1/4$" (20 x 26 cm)

* decorative or plain machine embroidery thread (optional) for the sole trim

* 3 pieces of corrugated cardboard, each $11^3/4$" (30 cm) square

* $^3/8$ yard ($^1/4$ m) rubber matting for the bottom of the Sole

* craft knife

* glue gun and glue sticks

* Summer Shoes Upper, Back, Fabric Sole and Sole pattern pieces (see pages 120–123)

NOTE: The materials listed above have enough fabric to make one pair of shoes.

1. Enlarge all the pattern pieces to full size. Use them to cut out the fabric pieces from the base fabric and the lining as follows:

Patched and pieced fabric: 2 Uppers and 2 Backs

Lining fabric: 2 Uppers, 2 Soles, 2 Backs, two 2" x 28" (5 x 71 cm) lengths for the Sole trim.

Wadding (batting): 2 Soles

Corrugated cardboard: 6 Soles

Rubber matting: 2 Soles

2. Glue wadding to one side of a cardboard Sole. Attach wadding to another cardboard Sole, making sure that it is shaped so that the set has a right foot and left foot.

3. Cover the wadding side of each of the Soles with a Fabric Sole, wrapping the edges to the underside, and gluing them in place on the outside edges (the underside) (**A**).

4. Using fusible webbing, join the wrong sides of a Back lining piece to a Back patched and pieced piece. If desired, satin stitch over cord filler along one long, curved edge. Make a second Back and two Uppers in the same way.

5. Glue a Back and then an Upper to each of the fabric-wrapped Soles, lining up the center of the Upper with the center front of the fabric-wrapped Sole, and the center of the Back with the center back of the fabric-wrapped Sole (**B**).

6. Sew satin-stitched piping or a line of decorative machine embroidery down the center of the strip of plain lining fabric (**C**).

7. Glue together the remaining Sole pieces: 2 right pieces joined back-to-back and 2 left pieces joined. Glue the embroidered sole trim around the edge of each joined Sole (**D**).

8. Glue the trimmed sole to each of the Soles that have the Upper and Back already attached to them.

9. Glue the rubber matting Sole to the bottom of each shoe.

When cutting out the Soles, remember to flip over the pattern piece before cutting out the second shape, so that you cut a right foot and a left foot. Rubber matting can be cut easily with a craft knife.

A

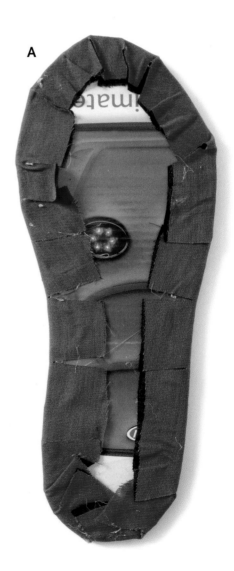

B

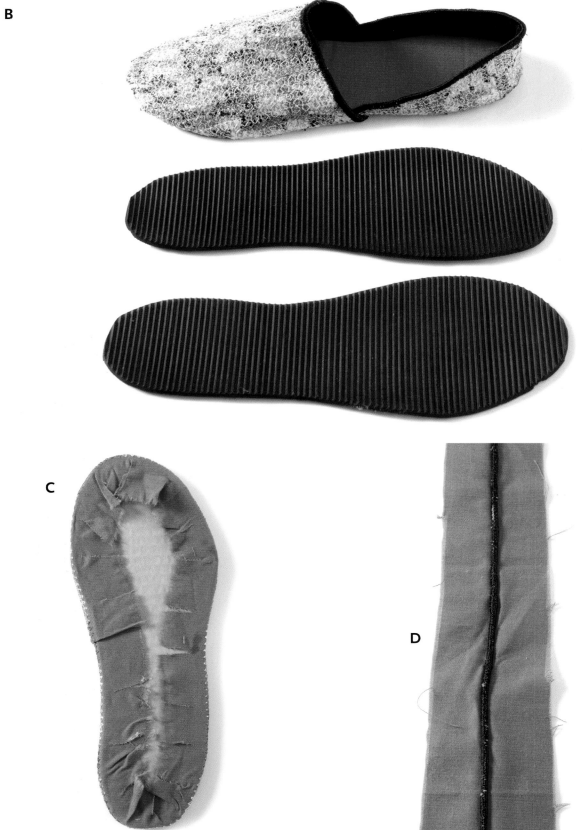

C

D

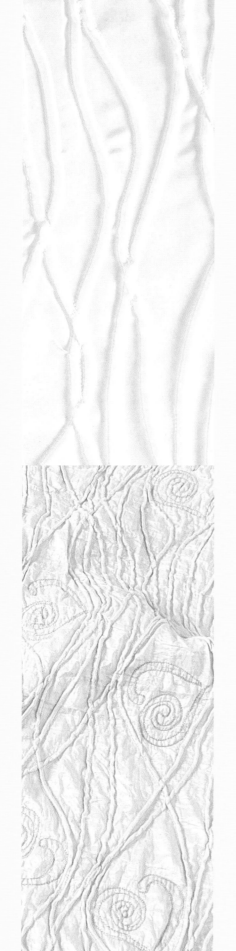

CHAPTER 6

Fabric Manipulation: Using the Structure

This chapter exploits the fact that some fabrics shrink. The projects and techniques presented on the following pages will show you how two fabrics can be combined by stitching them together and then shrinking them to create surface texture. Using wool gauze is a great way to texture fabric and still keep its original feel. The washing machine does all the work, and machine stitching can be used creatively to produce different effects. This chapter will also show how some synthetic fabrics shrink when direct heat, in the form of a heat gun, is applied to them. These fabrics will be used to create fabric beads, used in the necklace project in Chapter 3.

Texturing a Fabric Surface

Wool gauze is a very fine fabric that will shrink at temperatures of 104°F (40°C) and above, especially if the heat is combined with agitation. This characteristic makes the gauze ideal for creative exploration. When stitched as a backing to other fabrics that do not shrink and then run through a cycle in a washing machine, the wool will felt and shrink dramatically. This shrinkage pulls up the top fabric.

The following steps explain how to make this interesting fabric as well as check shrinkage before going ahead with a project.

MATERIALS

* wool gauze fabric
* fabric that is 100 percent synthetic or preshrunk
* natural or synthetic embroidery thread
* twin needle
* washing machine

1. Cut out a piece of wool gauze. When making samples to check shrinkage, use a fat quarter. Cut a yard (meter) of fabric in half, across both the length and width. Dividing fabric in this way gives a good size for a sample and avoids waste.

2. Cut a piece of fabric to the same size as the wool gauze and pin the two fabrics together with wrong sides facing. Measure and record the length and width of the combined fabric pieces.

3. Insert a twin needle into the machine. Use the machine embroidery thread in the bobbin and the needle. Stitch either in straight or wavy lines, through both fabric layers, across the entire surface (see samples at right). Experiment with the distance between each row of twin needle stitching to find the right distance for your taste.

4. Wash the fabric at 104°F (40°C) in the washing machine, running it through the entire cycle, using a nonbiological detergent. You will find that washing the sample with other fabrics increases the shrinkage.

5. Dry the fabric and measure the size. Compare this to the measurements of the original piece to determine the percentage of shrinkage you need to keep in mind when buying yardage for your project.

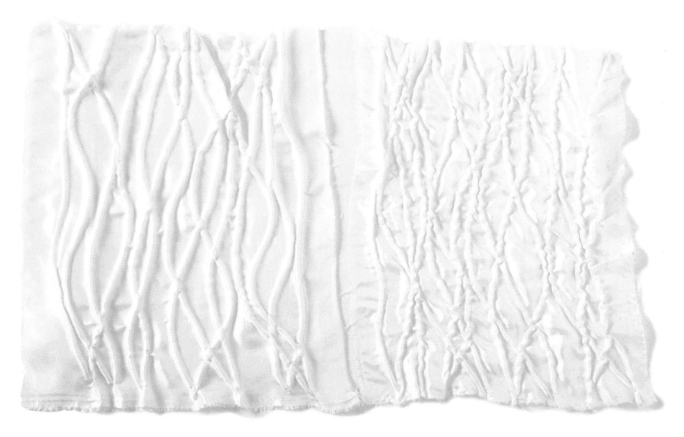

Fine cotton or preshrunk wool, polyester and silks make great top layers for this technique. The samples shown above were stitched with a 6.0/100 twin needle, but experiment with other sizes. The swatch to the left shows how the fabric looks before it is shrunk. The swatch at right shows the results.

TIPS

Be careful when stitching wavy lines, as it is very easy to break a twin needle.

Fabric shrinkage can be controlled by the direction and type of stitching, and also by the way that the fabric is washed after stitching. Drying in a tumble dryer will also add to the shrinkage.

The finished project can be laundered in a washing machine and dryer without worrying about additional shrinkage.

It is really important to do samples before starting a project using this technique, as it is impossible to estimate the shrinkage of different fabrics. Try to make samples for as many types of fabric as you can.

Fabric Beads

Fabric beads are great fun to make and are really useful for decorating items where glass or plastic beads are not practical. Synthetic fabrics combined with pattern stitches allow you to be really creative with texture and colour.

MATERIALS

* selection of 100 percent synthetic fabrics, plain and patterned (Note: Each bead requires only one fabric strip.)
* heat gun
* quilt pin with a glass head
* wooden skewer or bamboo knitting needle
* machine embroidery thread colour-matched to the fabrics

> **NOTE:** Madeira FS 2/2—also known as Madeira Metallic No. 20 Art FS 981—is a good choice as it does not burn easily. YLI Machine Quilting and Valdani Cotton Threads can also be used.

1. Tear or cut fabric into a strip approximately 1" (2.5 cm) wide. Tearing gives a better edge, but experiment with both tearing and cutting to find out which method you prefer.

2. Sew along the strip using a pattern stitch and a machine embroidery thread.

3. Cut the strip into lengths of approximately 3" (7.5 cm).

4. Wind each strip tightly around a wooden skewer and secure the end with a pin.

5. Heat the wrapped fabric with a heat gun for just a few seconds. The fabric will start to melt.

6. Switch off the gun and push the top and bottom edges of the bead toward each other. This will fatten the bead. Remove the pin and then quickly roll the bead between your fingers, while it is still on the wooden skewer. If you do this while the fabric is hot, the fabric forms and retains a bead shape. Slide the bead off the skewer.

Sheer and very lightweight fabrics give the best results. Work with a selection of patterned and plain colours.

It takes a bit of practice to master this technique, but you will soon learn the best fabrics to use. Experiment with different threads and stitches. Keep a record of your samples in a swatch folder, recording as much information as you can.

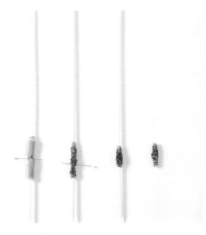

After embellishing a fabric strip, cut it into smaller lengths, wrap it around a wooden skewer and then melt and form it into its final shape.

To make a larger bead, start with a wider and longer fabric strip.

Always wear a respirator when burning any fabric with a heat gun.

Never let the heat gun burn the skewer. Make sure that it does not melt the fabric too much.

Work with your hand in a thin cotton glove if your fingers are sensitive to heat.

Decorate a soft bag with fabric beads.

Textured Vest

Simple shaping on this vest (known in the UK as a waistcoat) helps show-case the interesting surface. The fabric looks complex, but it is not difficult to make. Combine fine wool gauze and silk jersey fabric that has been dyed with indigo. Like the Swirl-Painted Wrap shown on page 56, this vest is made from one piece of fabric.

The finished size of your vest will depend on the amount of fabric you start with, as well as the amount that you allow the combined fabric yardage to shrink in the washing machine.

TIP

When the combined fabrics have been washed, the width will be reduced by one-third and the length by one-fifth. The shrinkage of your fabrics may be different, so always stitch a sample before deciding on the amount of fabric you need for your vest.

MATERIALS

* 1¹/₂ yards (1.5 m) each of 54" (135 cm) -wide fine wool gauze and bezique silk jersey (Note: The jersey can be dyed with indigo or left plain.)

* 1¹/₂ yards (1.5 m) of 54" (135 cm) -wide lining fabric, such as cotton dyed with indigo

* all-purpose sewing thread colour-matched to the silk jersey

* 6.0/100 twin needle or size of your choice

* single needle

* washing machine

* scissors

* pins

1. Cut out a fabric rectangle from the wool gauze to the size you need. For sizes 10–12 (UK 12–14) this will be approximately 27" x 49" (69 x 124 cm). For sizes 14–16 (UK 16–18), this will be approximately 32" x 49" (81 x 124 cm). This vest is designed to finish at the waist and these measurements are for this length. Add to the length at this point if needed.

2. Cut out a rectangle of bezique silk jersey to the same size as the wool gauze, making sure that you cut the fabric with the knit of the jersey running the length of the rectangle.

3. With the wrong sides together, pin the fabrics around the perimeter and sew all around the edges with a straight stitch and single needle. This perimeter stitching will hold the fabrics in place while the decorative stitch-ing is worked. This is not necessary on a small sample, as it is easy to keep the fabrics in place.

4. Insert the twin needle into the machine and stitch from the top to the bottom of the fabric. End the line of stitching (back stitching is not neces-sary at the beginning and end of the seam).

A

B

C

5. Turn the fabric layers and stitch from the bottom to the top, crossing the lines of stitching in places every few inches (**A**). Continue stitching up and down across the width of the fabric.

6. Wash the fabric at 104°F (40°C) in a washing machine. (See the technique on page 97 for additional advice on this process.)

7. Measure the finished yardage and cut out the lining to match (**B**). The vest is designed to finish at the waist, but you can make it longer or shorter if you wish.

8. Join the lining to the fabric with the wrong sides together and pin.

9. Stitch around the outside of the fabric with a dense, medium-width satin stitch (**C**). This joins the edges of the fabrics together and gives a decorative edge at the same time.

10. Mark the center of the fabric and make the opening for the neck and the front of the vest by following steps 1 and 2 of the Swirl-Painted Wrap on page 56.

11. Stitch around the front and neck edges with a dense, medium-width satin stitch. Stitch the side seams, leaving the top 9" (23 cm) open for the arms.

OPPOSITE
Knitted silk jersey is a gorgeous naturally coloured fabric that can be used without dyeing it. It will coordinate with any outfit.

Evening Shawl

Using fine wool gauze and either silk or polyester taffeta, it is easy to stitch an elegant shawl. This would be a perfect accessory for a wedding or an evening dress. It is important for the two featured fabrics to be the same width, as you will be using the entire width of the fabric as the length of the finished shawl.

TIP

The Evening Shawl should need straight lines of stitching only to finish off the short ends, but you could experiment with tassels or even fabric beads. Just be careful not to make the wrap too fussy.

MATERIALS

* ¹/₂ yard (¹/₂ m) of 54" (135 cm) -wide fine wool gauze for the base
* 1 yard (1 m) of 54" (135 cm) -wide silk or polyester taffeta for the surface and the lining
* all-purpose thread colour-matched to the fabric
* 6.0/100 twin needle
* single needle
* scissors
* pins

A

TAFFETA AND WOOL GAUZE LAYERS

1. Cut ¹/₂ yard (¹/₂ m) of the taffeta.

2. With the wrong sides together, pin together the wool gauze and the taffeta cut in step 1 and stitch around the outside edges (**A**).

B

C   RIGHT SIDE OF FABRIC

3. About $3/4$" (1.9 cm) from one short end, sew across the width of the fabric. Turn the fabric and sew along the width again, about a presser foot width from the first line of stitching (**B**). Continue sewing up and down the fabric width until the entire surface is covered. Make the last line of stitching about $3/4$" (1.9 cm) from the edge.

4. Wash the stitched fabric at 104°F (40°C) to shrink it as desired. (See the technique on page 97 for additional advice on this process.)

5. Measure the finished fabric and cut a piece of taffeta fabric to the same dimensions, for the lining.

6. Change the sewing machine needle to a single needle. With right sides together, stitch the lining to the main fabric with an overcast stitch and $5/8$" (15 mm) seam allowance, leaving a gap of approximately 2" (5 cm) in the center of one end.

7. Turn the shawl to the right side. Turn under the edges of the gap and pin them in place.

8. Top stitch across both ends of the shawl with medium-length straight stitches and the first line of stitching very close to the edge (**C**). This will close the gap. Remove the pins.

9. Stitch with two more lines of single-row straight stitching to finish the shawl's short ends.

LEFT
Try incorporating a motif into the stitching. The shawl to the left was made for a wedding, so it has a heart motif that was created with free-motion embroidery. The twin-needle stitching was worked around the motifs.

Use a commercially printed fabric stitched with metallic thread to make an elegant evening shawl.

GALLERY

Tea for Two

This coat was created by Sue Ackerman of South Africa. Sue is a textile artist and author of the book Wearable Dreams Out of Africa. *Her coat is made from tea bags and machine embroidered with the names of friends around the world she wishes she could have tea with . . . including the author.*

Corset for Mrs. Midas

Called Corset for Mrs. Midas, *this piece is from a series called Corsets for the Wives of Famous Men. It shows how dissolved Kunin felt can be used for garments. The corset was stitched on beige felt with digitized motifs and free-motion machine embroidery. Part of the corset was sprayed with gold acrylic paint.*

Victorian Miss Shoes

These shoes were made from a base fabric of vintage Sea Island cotton that was designed by my grandfather. Antique lace was applied to this base and the fabric was then decorated with machine embroidery and antique pearls.

Black Magic

Make a glitzy evening bag using metallic candy wrappers. This is a structured bag that is intended for occasional use only, as it is only glued together! Structured bags are normally constructed on an industrial cylinder arm machine. This construction is not possible on a domestic machine as the free arm is too big. A glue gun will bond components together with an almost-instantaneous strong bond, but any strong fabric glue can be used. If you need your bag to be stronger, it is possible to hand stitch it together with a leather needle, but it is hard work!

Vintage Lace

This very pretty Victorian-style corset was stitched on scraps of old lace. The corset closes with a busk fastening and has false laces on the back panel. I have decorated mine with pearls from an old broken necklace. You could antique new lace with walnut ink and use beads to create motifs or to trim the top and bottom edges. Experiment!

Seaside Jacket

The design for this jacket is based on lettering forms that are linked to a project about the seaside. Bleach was sponged through a stencil onto the black cotton fabric. The fabric was rinsed to stop the bleach action and remove any residue. The patterns were embellished using free-motion embroidery and a range of black and gold decorative threads. This jacket was created by Viv White.

Patterns

Corset Jacket

(see page 33)
Enlarge all pieces by 400%

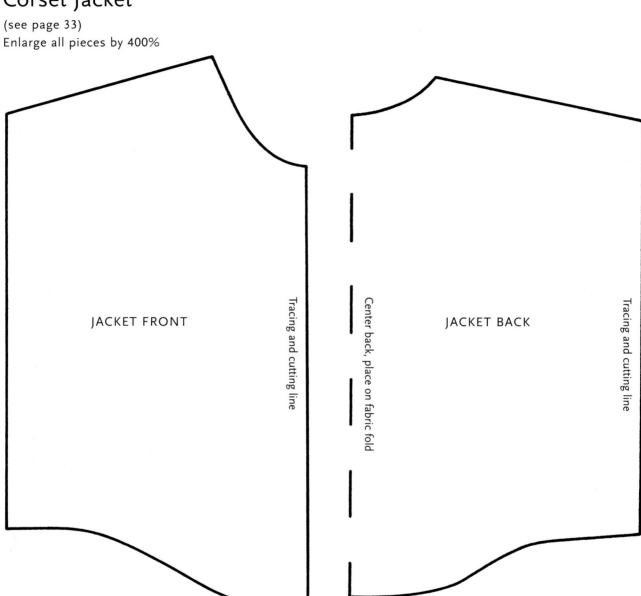

JACKET FRONT

Tracing and cutting line

Center back, place on fabric fold

JACKET BACK

Tracing and cutting line

Jacket Front:

Cut 2 from base fabric and 2 from lining

Jacket Back:

Cut 1 from base fabric and 1 from lining

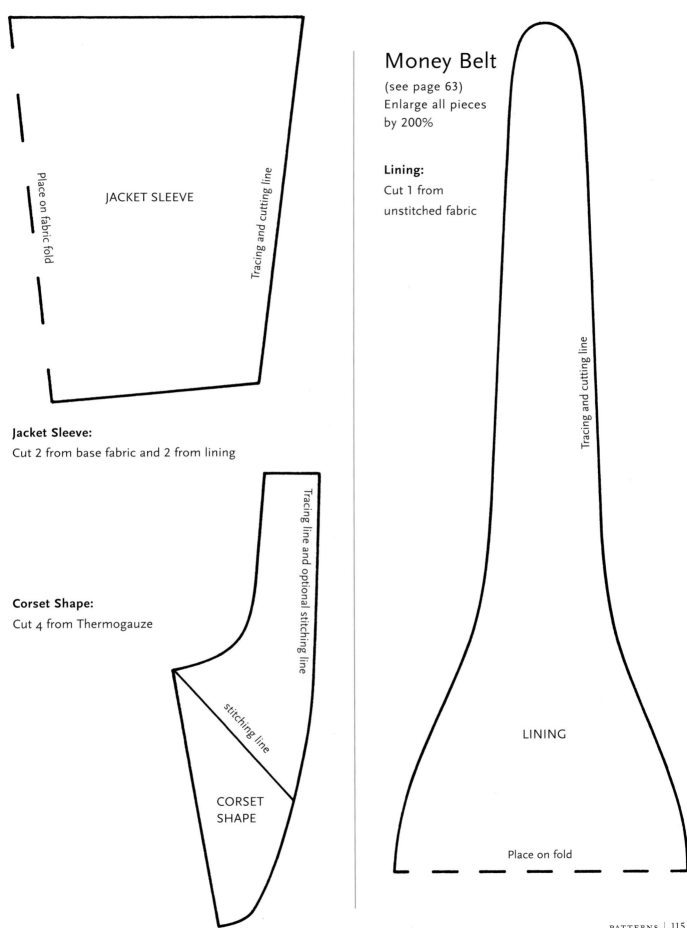

JACKET SLEEVE

Place on fabric fold

Tracing and cutting line

Jacket Sleeve:
Cut 2 from base fabric and 2 from lining

Corset Shape:
Cut 4 from Thermogauze

Tracing line and optional stitching line

stitching line

CORSET
SHAPE

Money Belt

(see page 63)
Enlarge all pieces
by 200%

Lining:
Cut 1 from
unstitched fabric

Tracing and cutting line

LINING

Place on fold

Money Belt (continued)

(see page 63)

Enlarge all pieces by 200%

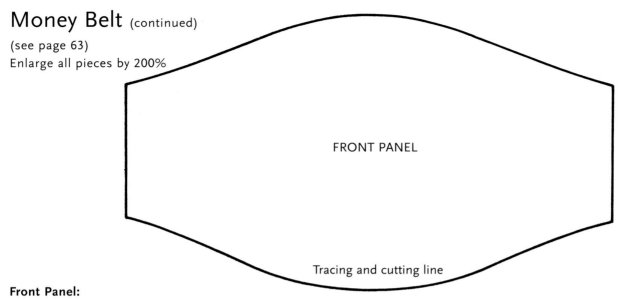

FRONT PANEL

Tracing and cutting line

Front Panel:

Cut 1 from stitched fabric, cut 2 from plain fabric

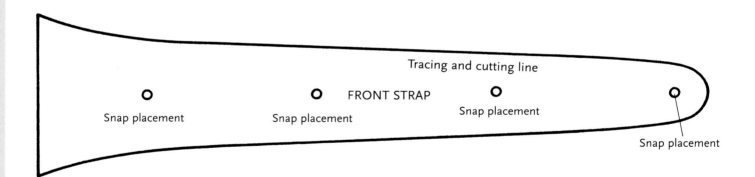

Tracing and cutting line

Snap placement   Snap placement   FRONT STRAP   Snap placement   Snap placement

Front Strap:

Cut 2 from plain fabric

T-Shape Soft Bag

(see page 75)
Enlarge all pieces by 200%

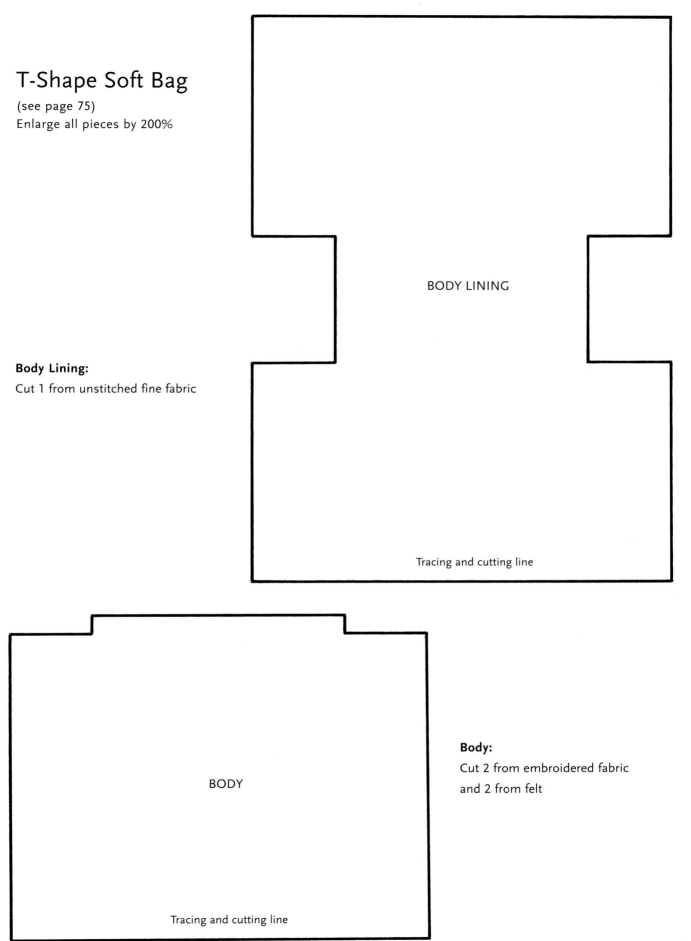

BODY LINING

Body Lining:
Cut 1 from unstitched fine fabric

Tracing and cutting line

BODY

Body:
Cut 2 from embroidered fabric
and 2 from felt

Tracing and cutting line

T-Shape Soft Bag (continued)

(see page 75)
Enlarge all pieces by 200%

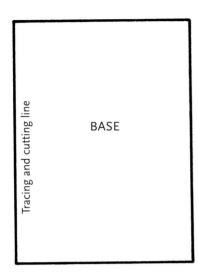

Base:

Cut 1 from felt, 1 from
fusible webbing,
and 1 from unstitched
fine fabric

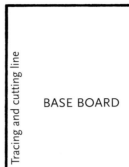

Base Board:

Cut 1 from card stock

Handle:

Cut 2 from unstitched fine fabric and 2 from felt

HANDLE

Tracing and cutting line

Facing:

Cut 2 from embroidered fabric

FACING

Catch placement

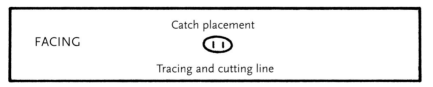

Tracing and cutting line

Handle Lining:

Cut 2 from unstitched fine fabric and 2 from felt

HANDLE LINING

Tracing and cutting line

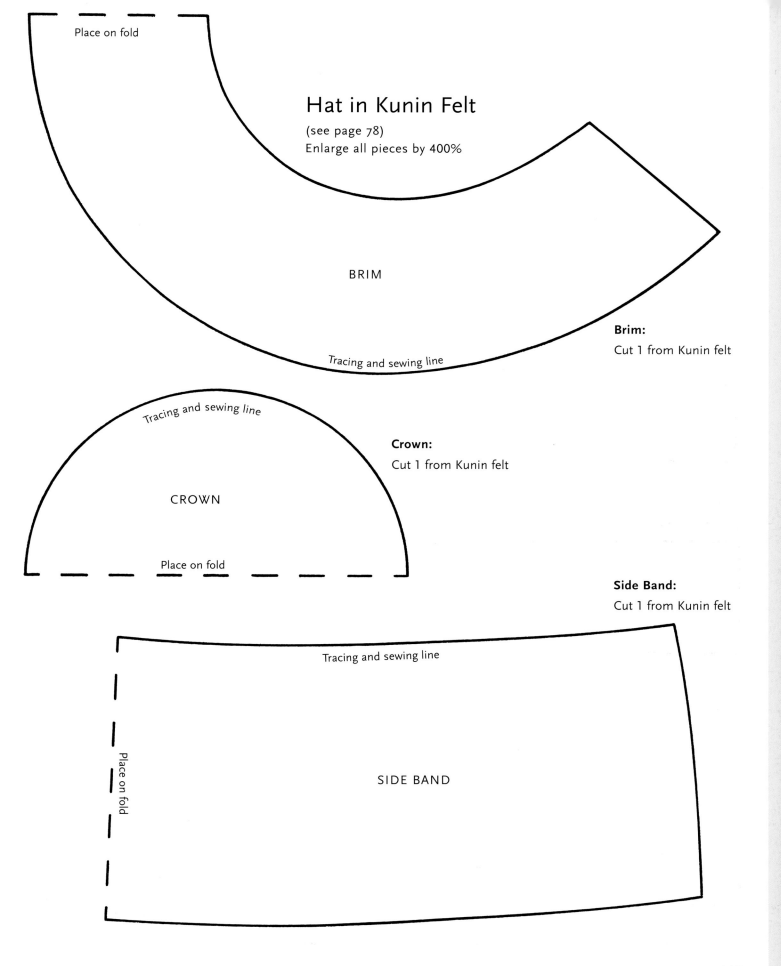

Place on fold

Hat in Kunin Felt

(see page 78)
Enlarge all pieces by 400%

BRIM

Tracing and sewing line

Brim:
Cut 1 from Kunin felt

Tracing and sewing line

CROWN

Place on fold

Crown:
Cut 1 from Kunin felt

Side Band:
Cut 1 from Kunin felt

Tracing and sewing line

Place on fold

SIDE BAND

Glitzy Belt

(see page 81)
Patterns shown at actual size

Tracing lines

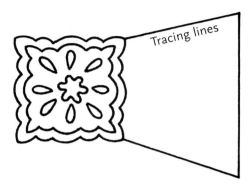

Tracing lines

Motif:
Trace on length of Romeo 10 times, with gaps between motifs; trace 2 outer lines on second length of Romeo, with gaps between motifs

Catch Motif:
Trace on right end of length of Romeo with motifs

Summer Shoes

(see page 91)
Enlarge all pieces by 200%

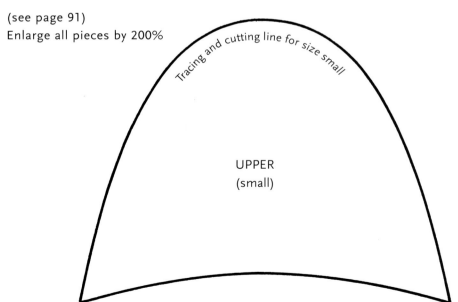

Tracing and cutting line for size small

UPPER
(small)

Upper:
Cut 2 from patched and pieced fabric; cut 2 from lining

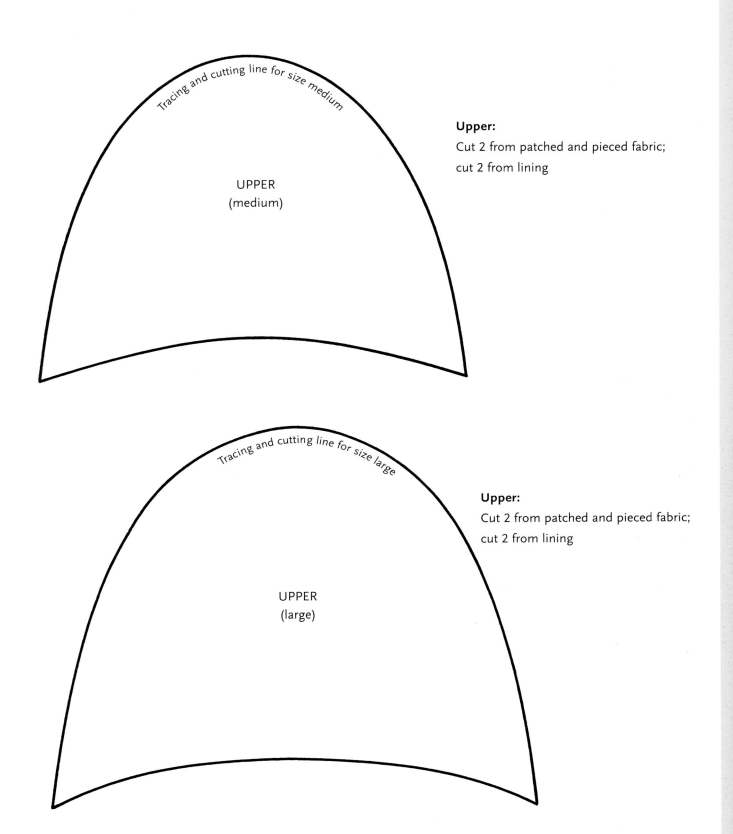

Tracing and cutting line for size medium

UPPER
(medium)

Upper:
Cut 2 from patched and pieced fabric;
cut 2 from lining

Tracing and cutting line for size large

UPPER
(large)

Upper:
Cut 2 from patched and pieced fabric;
cut 2 from lining

Summer Shoes (continued)

(see page 91)
Enlarge all pieces by 200%

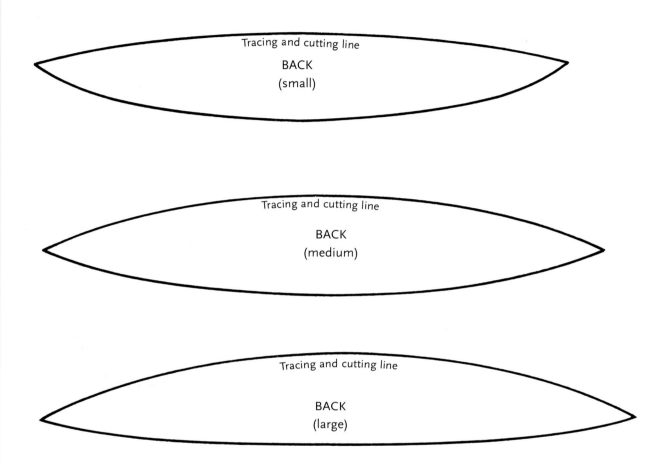

Back:

Cut 2 from patched and pieced fabric, cut 2 from lining

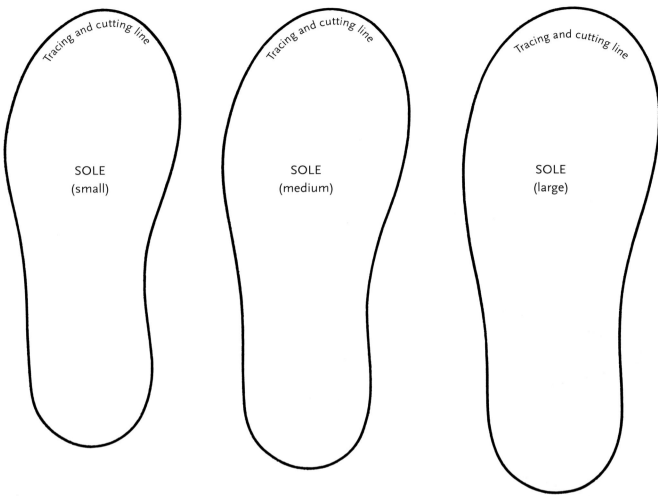

Sole:

Cut 2 from lining, cut 2 from wadding (batting), cut 6 from corrugated cardboard, cut 2 from rubber matting

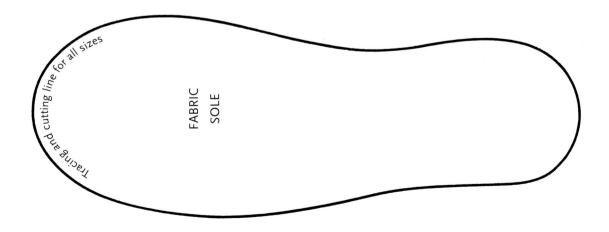

Fabric Sole:

Cut 2 from lining

RESOURCES

UNITED KINGDOM

Barnyarns LTD
Canal Wharf, Bondgate Green
Ripon, North Yorkshire HG4 1AQ
08708 708 586
international +44-1765-690069
www.barnyarns.com
Madeira threads

Fibrecrafts (George Weil & Sons Ltd)
Old Portsmouth Rd.
Peasemarsh, Guildford
Surrey GU3 1LZ
14835 658 00
www.fibercrafts.com
*Alum, indigo, Jaquard Dye-Na-Flow paints,
transfer paints, crayons*

French Knot Studio
32 Old Manor Way
Drayton, Portsmouth PO6 2NN
02392 326 408
www.frenchknotstudio.co.uk
Valdani threads

Gillsew
Boundary House, Moor Common
Lane End, Bucks HP14 3HR
01494 881 886
email: gillsew@ukonlline.co.uk
Printing blocks (stamps), threads

Ivy House Studio
37 High St.
Kessingland, Suffolk WR33 7QQ
01502 740 414
www.ivyhousestudio.com
*Aquatics Romeo Soluble Film, glue guns,
heat guns, hot water-soluble fabric, Kunin felt,
walnut ink*

Kemtex Colours
Chorley Business & Technology Centre
Euxton Ln.
Chorley, Lancashire PR7 6TE
01257 230 220
www.kemtex.co.uk
Indigo dye

Kleins
5 Noel St.
London W1F 8GD
02074 876 162
www.kleins.co.uk
*Corset supplies, handbag notions,
sew-in magnets*

Prescott & Mackay
74 Broadway Market
London E8 4QJ
02079 239 450
www.prescottandmackay.co.uk
*Courses in shoemaking in the United Kingdom
and the United States*

The India Shop
5 Hilliers Yard
Marlborough, Wilts SN8 1BE
01672 851 155
www.theindiashop.co.uk
*Fabric patchwork pieces, printing blocks
(stamps)*

Whaleys (Bradford) Ltd.
Harris Court, Great Horton,
Bradford, West Yorkshire BD7 4EQ
01274 576 718
www.whaleys-bradford.ltd.uk
Mail-order silk jersey, muslin cotton, wool gauze

Winifred Cottage
17 Elms Rd.
Fleet, Hants. GU51 3EG
01252 617 667
email: WinifCott@aol.com
*Aquatics Romeo Soluble Film, hot water–soluble
fabric, Madeira threads, Thermogauze*

UNITED STATES

Dharma Trading Co.
P.O. Box 150916
San Rafael, CA 94915
800-542-5227
www.dharmatrading.com
Cottons, indigo dye, silks

Dick Blick Art Materials
P.O. Box 1267
Galesburg, IL 61402
800-828-4548
www.dickblick.com
Glue gun, heat gun

DC Enterprises
P.O. Box 15743
Philadelphia, PA 19103
215-868-4274
www.corsetmaking.com
Corset supplies

Kunin Felt
380 Lafayette Rd.
Hampton, NH 03843
800-292-7900
www.kuninfelt.com
Kunin felt products

MeinkeToy LLC
55 East Long Lake Rd.
Troy, MI 48085
www.meinketoy.com
Thermogauze, threads

Rags-n-Tags
Kristal Norton
27 Faith Rd.
Newington CT 06111
www.rags-n-tags.com
walnut ink

RnL Lee
P.O. Box 1032
Bethlehem, PA 18016
610-691-7728
www.rnllee.com
Handbag supplies

Rupert, Gibbon & Spider Inc
P.O. Box 425
Healdsburg, CA 95448
800-442-0455
www.jacquardproducts.com
Jacquard Dye-Na-Flow paints, silks

AUSTRALIA & NEW ZEALAND

Accent Fibres
1084 Maraekakaho Rd.
R.D. 5
Hastings, Hawkes Bay
New Zealand
+64-6-876-4233
www.dyepot.co.nz
Jacquard paints, Thermogauze

Batik Oetoro
203 Avoca St.
Randwick, NSW 2031
Australia
+61-2-9398-6201
www.dyeman.com
Indigo dyes

Nicole Mallalieu Design
P.O. Box 298
Brunswick Vic 3056
Australia
+61-(03) 9940-1533
www.nicolemdesign.com.au
Handbag supplies

The Thread Studio
6 Smith St.
Perth 6000
Western Australia
+61-8-9227-1561
www.thethreadstudio.com
Thermogauze, Victory Embroidery Thread

Unique impressions
Shop 6, Arcadia Walk
Noosa Junction, Queensland 4567
Australia.
+61-07-5449-2835
www.uniqueimpressions.com.au
Jacquard paints

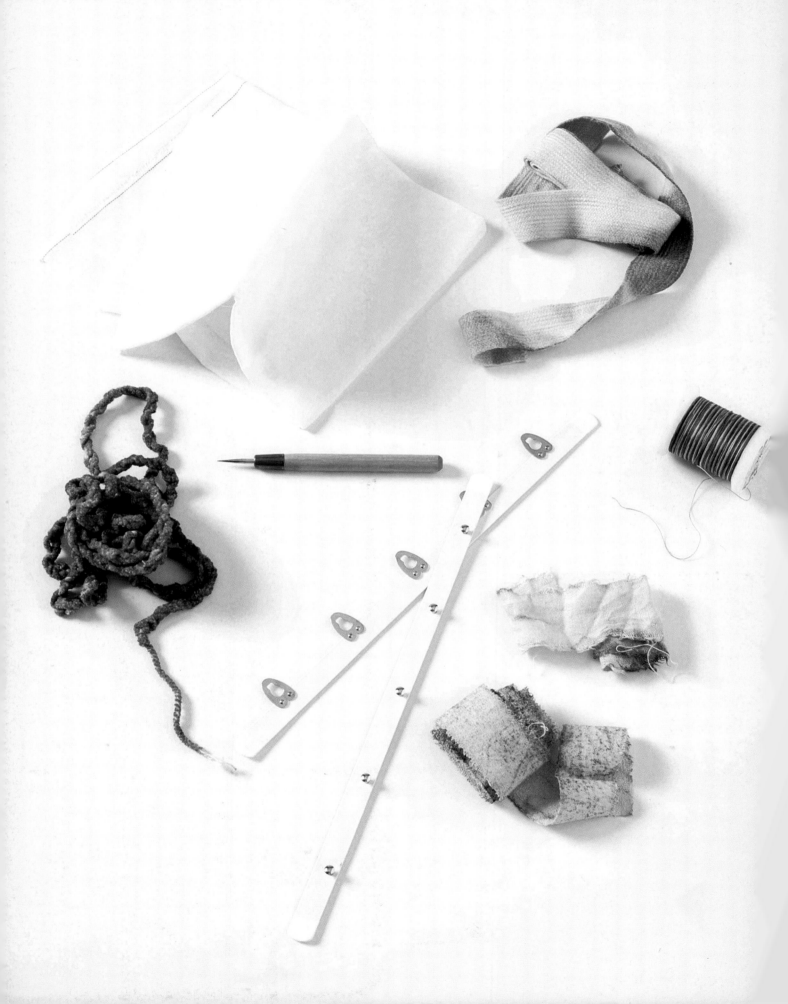

ABOUT THE AUTHOR

Elli Woodsford, MSDC, has a studio in Hampshire, England, where she teaches machine embroidery and textile decoration. A member of the Society of Designer Craftsmen and holder of a City & Guilds Medal for Excellence for Automatic Decorative Stitching, her work explores the creation of unique surface design applications on fabrics for use in clothing and accessories. Her website is www.embexstudio.com.

ACKNOWLEDGMENTS

I would like to thank the Quarry Books staff for their help and encouragement, particularly my editor Mary Ann Hall for always being so efficient.

Also, thanks to my copy editor and technical editor, Susan Huxley, whose knowledge and sense of humor have been invaluable.

Thank you also to the following people:

My family, for being so patient

My first embroidery tutor, textile artist Brenda Weeks, for being so inspirational

The members of FibreWorks Textile Group, for new goals

My students, for enthusiasm

My greatest friend and mentor, textile artist Barbara Taylor, who tested every project in this book, and whose artistic ability and sense of colour always inspires

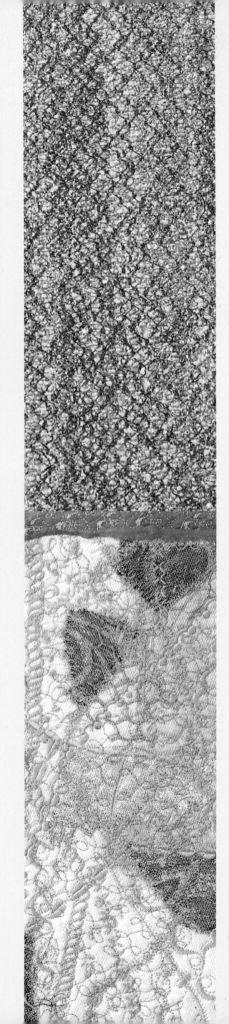